THREE SISTERS

THREE SISTERS

MICHAEL HARPER

A provocative look
at Evangelicals, Charismatics,
& Catholic Charismatics
and their relationship
to one another

Tyndale House
Publishers, Inc.
Wheaton, Illinois

LIBRARY OF CONGRESS CATALOG CARD NUMBER 78-57960
ISBN 0-8423-7145-1
COPYRIGHT © 1979 BY MICHAEL HARPER.
FIRST PRINTING, MARCH 1979.
PRINTED IN THE UNITED STATES OF AMERICA

CONTENTS

Thank yous

There are many to whom I'm grateful for help in the writing of this book. Of course, as the reader will soon discover, it would have been impossible without the friendship of evangelicals, who introduced me to Jesus as Lord; of Pentecostals and charismatics, who have taught me many lessons in walking in the Spirit; and of Roman Catholics, who have helped me to see that church history did not begin at the reformation, nor will end without a unity with them and others which I would neither have believed possible or even desirable a few years back.

I would like to thank Larry Christenson, whose friendship has meant so much to me, for his reading of the section on "discipleship" and for his comments and suggested alterations.

Thanks also to Church Society and to Fountain Trust for allowing me to reprint the material in Appendix B.

And thank you, Norah Garratt, for typing the manuscript so beautifully and for all your help, without which the book could not have been finished. And thanks to Nita Downe for typing the appendices.

I always seem to finish books these days at significant moments! This one was completed on Good Friday. Thanks be to God for sending his Son and for the Christ of Calvary who through the Cross has reconciled men to God *and to one another*, thus making Christian unity possible. Christ prayed that we would be "of one heart and mind, just as you and I are, Father" (John 17:21, *The Living Bible*). The Psalmist tells us: "It was the stone rejected by the builders that proved to be the keystone; this is Yahweh's doing and it is wonderful to see. This is the day made memorable by Yahweh, what immense joy for us! . . . Yahweh is God, he smiles on us" (Psalm 118:22-24, 27, *Jerusalem Bible*). Surely he is smiling on every way in which his people are discovering unity in his Son.

Michael Harper
Good Friday 1978
Hounslow   Middlesex

7

ONE
MEETING THREE
SISTERS:
A Love Story

This book is about three sisters. I met them one by one. In fact, my whole life has been radically influenced by them. I met the first member of the family while I was studying law at Cambridge University. You could say that it was a chance encounter, or that my whole life had been a preparation for it. In a sense both were true. Her name was Evangeline, and if I had not met her I would almost certainly not have met the other sisters. But then again, it is now clear that Evangeline was not at all anxious that I should meet her sisters, but kept strangely secretive about them.

I owe my Christian conversion to Evangeline. I was so captivated by this remarkable woman that to begin with I was not the least bit interested in the rest of the family. Evangeline changed the whole course of my life. She taught me that it is possible to know God and that the basis of Christian life is a personal relationship with Jesus Christ. She assured me that the Bible was trustworthy and helped me both to understand and love it. In many ways she was more a mother to me than a sister. She introduced me to many of her friends, and I was content to keep to the friendly circle that revolved around her and to accept her views unconditionally. I really wasn't interested in the rest of her family.

I did occasionally encounter the other sisters; but I could tell from the worried frown on Evangeline's face that these could at best be only brief encounters, and that it would be better if we didn't meet at all. Occasionally she would let me see books written against her two sisters, and I remember being indignant that they should dare to claim to be part of the same family, although I was later to discover that the pictures painted in those books were often grotesque caricatures.

But in 1962 I really got to know the second sister, whose name was Charisma. I was working for the family business at the time, or rather Evangeline's part of that business. It was doing really well and I was happy to be part of the life of one of the largest branches of the business. Charisma was quite different from Evangeline. My meeting with her had a clandestine element to it, for I soon discovered that Evangeline and Charisma were not on speaking terms with one another. I was tempted at times to think she might even be "illegitimate" or at best only a half-sister. But time was to prove otherwise.

Unfortunately, Evangeline took strong exception to my friendship with Charisma and a deep rift swiftly developed. I found that Evangeline's friends were not so happy to see me now. I began to be treated as a renegade and my reputation became badly tarnished. They seemed now to be very suspicious of me. I was eyed with sorrow.

Some years later I met Roma, the third sister. Again there was something distinctly secretive about the meeting. But in contrast to Charisma, who was almost totally unknown to me before I met her, I had known about Roma for many years. I had even heard about her before I met Evangeline. But I had strenuously avoided any form of encounter. The main reason was that she had such a bad reputation. Some of Evangeline's friends actually called her a "whore," and some of the people I met through Charisma used to hide their faces with shame and prophesy against Roma.

I was surprised, therefore, when eventually I met her, that she was related to the other sisters, and was chaste. As I got to know her better, I found she was not nearly as bad as some of my earlier friends had suggested, and had much more in common with the other sisters than I had ever thought possible. In fact, when the three sisters were together I was always at my happiest and found it hard to understand why they had stayed apart for so long. They seemed to complement each other so perfectly.

Anthony Sampson has written a fascinating book about business corporations that somewhat dominate our present world—seven major world oil companies: Texaco, Shell, Mobil, British Petroleum, Standard Oil, Chevron, and Gulf. He has called the book *The Seven Sisters*.[1] My book is about three major influences in the contemporary Church. They are spiritual bodies which are at the moment pursuing separate courses. I owe a great debt of gratitude to all three. To the Evangelical sister for teaching me the gospel and introducing me to Jesus Christ. To the Pentecostal sister for helping me to experience the spiritual dynamic of the Holy Spirit and to explore many neglected areas of the Holy Spirit's activity in the Church and the world. To the Catholic sister for ushering me into a whole new world where I could understand the more corporate dimensions of Christian life and learn to balance the spiritual with the human aspects of Christian truth (the Cross and the Incarnation, the Word and Sacraments, etc.).

I must confess to a deep longing to see these sisters reconciled to each other; to see them openly united in Christ and the Spirit, learning from one another and humbly listening to each other. If these sisters could be brought together on a large scale, there is no knowing the blessings that could follow.

In 1971 I became involved in the first concerted efforts at reconciling the second and third sisters. In that year preliminary discussions were held in Rome between the Secretariat for Promoting Christian Unity of the Roman Catholic Church, leaders of the charismatic movement in the historic churches, and leaders of some of the Pentecostal churches. I was privileged to be a member of the core group which planned the whole series of meetings which were held from 1972 to 1976, the results of which may be found in Appendix A (page 109).

In 1974 I also became involved in setting up a dialogue

11

between the first and second sisters. I had on several occasions suggested meetings to discuss differences of opinion between evangelicals and charismatics. The Fountain Trust (charismatics) and the Evangelical Alliance in Britain did meet on one or two occasions, but Anglican evangelicals declined such advances from our side until 1974. In that year the Fountain Trust celebrated its tenth anniversary, and I was invited to write an article for the Church of England newspaper. In it I again drew attention to the "charismatic divide" which existed then between Anglican evangelicals and charismatics, and I pleaded for the setting up of dialogue with a view to reconciling differences and overcoming estrangements and misunderstandings. I also wrote to John Stott asking him personally if this could be done.

There was a prompt and encouraging response. The Church of England Evangelical Council, under the chairmanship of John Stott, had met and supported positive steps toward reconciliation through dialogue. The first meeting was convened shortly afterwards at Swanwick in Derbyshire. From 1974 to 1977 Anglican evangelical leaders on both sides of the charismatic divide met, and the results of their discussion can be found in Appendix B (page 123).

This book is written with the sincere prayer that what has already taken place in terms of drawing together the three sisters may be consolidated, and that further steps will be taken so that the drawing together can have larger and more international dimensions. In 1977 in Venice, Italy, a further move was taken when conservative evangelicals for the first time began to dialogue with Roman Catholics. So all three sisters have begun to talk together at various levels and places. The three sisters constitute important influences in the worldwide Church.

The evangelical world is influencing the Church on every continent, and in many areas is experiencing an impressive resurgence. The Roman Catholic Church is far and away the largest in the world, and its ascendancy is still being felt in many parts of that world. Although its authority in some parts of the world has and is continuing to decline, in others, especially since the Church's commitment to *aggiornamento* (bringing up to date; modernization) through the second Vatican Council, that influence is growing. The Pentecostal or charismatic sister in many ways is the baby of the family, in some senses a bit of an afterthought, born long after the other two sisters. But it has one striking element which means that its influence is greater than its size—it has deeply and fully penetrated into both the evangelical and Roman Catholic kingdoms, and thus has a unique and important role as a bridge between the two.

It is very much easier for evangelical Christians, traditionally suspicious and hostile to the Papacy, to share with Roman Catholics when they have seen so many of these Roman Catholics deeply influenced by the charismatic movement in the direction of a more clearly articulated evangelical faith. Thus, my charismatic sister is being much used to bring the other two sisters together. Greater unity between the three would be bound to have a striking effect on the worldwide Church and its mission to mankind.

My evangelical sister was very British. I knew very little about American evangelicalism, one of the most dominant influences on the birth of that nation and on her resulting culture. I heard Billy Graham and was impressed. I heard about the "Bible belt" and it sounded scary. But my charismatic and Catholic sisters spoke very much with an American accent. I owe more than I can say to my American friends, who taught me so much about what the word "charismatic" was all about. I refer to people like David duPlessis, Larry Christenson, Frank Maguire, Dennis Bennett, Graham Pulkingham, and many others. And when I came to meet the Catholic world, it was a layman raised in the Bronx, Kevin Ranaghan, who helped so much. Many of my Catholic friends are Americans. It has been a privilege to work for five years in a dialogue with Kilian McDonnell, that most gifted and gracious charismatic ambassador from Collegeville, Minnesota, and also to know men like Ralph Martin and Francis MacNutt. I have felt a sense of deep brotherhood with them all.

The widespread move of the Holy Spirit in the United

States has been one of the most important events of the twentieth century. I think it will go down in history as the greatest revival in the 200 years plus of the United States, eclipsing in size and influence the great evangelical awakenings of the eighteenth and nineteenth centuries. I believe it will leave a permanent imprint on the nation. It happened at a time when America's worldwide reputation had hit an all-time low. The hopes of the short-lived Kennedy administration, shattered by an assassin's bullet in Dallas, Texas, were followed by the Vietnam disaster and the Watergate scandal. Americans were spat on in the streets of European cities. Embassies were attacked. In Stockholm, American property had to be guarded by police night and day. People everywhere began to believe that America was in deep trouble.

I visited the New World for the first time in 1965, taking Pan-Am into Chicago. I was to return many times in the coming years. I looked everywhere for the confirmation of my prejudices. I was not kept waiting long. The first night, while being driven home from a meeting, I spotted a bullet-riddled limousine parked on a side road. After all, this was Chicago. Southern California confirmed a few more prejudices. Americans *are* crazy, mixed-up people. They are rich, and too interested in making money. Most Europeans think of Americans as trigger-happy cowboys (the TV image) or loudly dressed, loud-speaking shutterbugs (the tourist image). That's how our prejudices are formed. And that's the America I thought I was going to see in 1965.

My prejudices were gradually dissolved. I think I have come to know the real American. Underneath the outward façade, which can be offensive to some, I have found a large-hearted and generous people. I have discovered integrity and kindness. We British have our own cultural clothing, which can be equally offensive and hurtful to Americans. I refer to the cold, formal, phlegmatic exterior of most English people. But I have found Americans to be, on the whole, a good deal more accepting and forgiving of our strange manners than we are of the American character. I have come to love America and Americans.

The charismatic movement owes a great deal to American inspiration and leadership. The United States is not finished. Out of the holocaust of Vietnam and the shame of Watergate is coming a new nation, and a crucial strand in the renewal of the nation has undoubtedly been the charismatic movement. We have not seen anything like this yet in most of the rest of the world.

It has been my pleasure to see many facets of the American charismatic scene. I have been in close touch with the Roman Catholic renewal, and have spoken at the massive National Conference in South Bend (in 1976). I have often been the guest of the Melodyland work of Ralph Wilkerson in Anaheim, California. I have spoken at Presbyterian and Episcopal national conferences. I have lectured at Oral Roberts University, and have written a book about the Church of the Redeemer, Houston, Texas (*A New Way of Living*). I have stayed in many homes across the nation. I love America. And this book is written with the hope and prayer that my charismatic sister will draw closer and closer to the two other sisters, the evangelical and Catholic worlds. But we need to look a little more closely at the three sisters.

TWO
THE EVANGELICAL
SCENE

It was in the spring of 1951 that I was introduced to the evangelical world. A few undergraduate friends began to evangelize me with genuine love and a sacrificial concern that was very moving. My conversion at Cambridge was thoroughly evangelical, apart from the fact that it took place in a Communion Service under the fan-vaulted ceiling of that famous tourist attraction, King's College Chapel.

But from then onwards it was evangelicalism all the way. I knew nothing else. I was taken shopping by my Christian friends for my first Bible. (It had to be the Scofield Reference Bible. And so I was introduced to dispensational fundamentalism.) I was urged to go to the Keswick Convention. I read the evangelical classics and sat at the feet of the famous evangelical preachers of the day.

Of course, evangelicalism is itself composed of different parts. This has always been true, and evangelicals have taken different positions on such thorny issues as Calvinism vs. Arminianism, water baptism, and prophecy. In the United States this has led to deep, and at times bitter, conflict between various factions. The controversies raised by modernism in the nineteenth century concerning the infallibility of the Bible, and by ecumenism in the twentieth century concerning Christian

17

unity and cooperation between Christians, were cataclysmic in their effects.

The appearance, beginning in 1910, of ten small volumes entitled *Fundamentals: A Testimony to the Truth*, edited by Amzi Dixon and Reuben Archer Torrey, caused a considerable stir. Over a period of several years, they were sent to over three million Christian leaders and workers, the enormous costs being borne by two wealthy Los Angeles businessmen, Milton and Lyman Stewart. Gradually a new word came into the church vocabulary, fundamentalist, that term first being used by a newspaperman, E. Laws, in 1920. The swords were being sharpened for the internecine struggle which took place in the 1920's and 30's, which was to split the evangelical world. After Harry Emerson Fosdick made the issues public, the matter came even more to a head through J. Gresham Machen, a scholarly Presbyterian from Princeton Theological Seminary. He was expelled from the Presbyterian Church in 1936, but died suddenly the following year. The limelight now shone on another Presbyterian who formed a different group from that of Machen's. He has been a strong force in the fundamentalist camp ever since. His name is Carl McIntire.

There was further controversy in the 1930's with the emergence of what came to be called neoorthodoxy. It was associated chiefly with the names of Karl Barth and Emil Brunner in Europe and Reinhold Niebuhr in the United States. Most evangelicals repudiated the teachings of these men.

But there were a growing number of people who, while going along with the fundamentalists in their attitudes to the Scriptures and the so-called "fundamentals" of the faith, did not want to be identified with some aspects of their teaching— for instance, their insistence on the premillennial view of the Second Coming—and could not go along with their literalistic interpretation of the Scriptures. There was also the beginning of an acceptance of some aspects of the so-called social gospel, which fundamentalism had up till then for the most part rejected. An increasing number of Bible-believing Christians were sickened by the aggressive denunciations of other Christians which poured out from fundamentalist sources, and could no longer accept the exclusive stances which were being taken and the attacks which were continuously being made on denominations in general—with the Roman Catholic Church as the chief target.

Thus, in the United States a new grouping began to take place, which began to use the term "evangelical" in contradistinction to that of "fundamentalist." One leader of this rising tide of "new look" evangelicalism was Harold John Ockenga, but one of its most prominent exponents was Billy Graham. The magazine *Christianity Today*, founded in 1956, did a great deal to promote this new evangelicalism. The new evangelicals found in Carl Henry, CT's first editor, a voice to speak the new evangelical language. They were eventually to find their greatest moment in the Lausanne Congress on Evangelism in 1974. But more about that later.

Richard Quebedeaux has described these developments in his important and informative book *The Young Evangelicals*.[2] He distinguishes between separatist fundamentalism (led by men like Carl McIntire and Billy James Hargis and served by institutions like Bob Jones University) and open fundamentalism (the tradition associated with Reuben Archer Torrey, in the tradition of Dwight L. Moody, and continued in the ministry of Billy Graham). Open fundamentalism would share with separatist fundamentalism a great many of its interpretations of the Bible, but it would take a much more open stance on issues such as ecumenism. Richard Quebedeaux further distinguishes what he calls establishment evangelicalism from both separatist fundamentalism and open fundamentalism. This has been largely a post-World War II development in the United States and would be represented by institutions such as Asbury Theological Seminary, Wheaton College, and Fuller Theological Seminary, and churches such as the Southern Baptist Convention (Billy Graham's own affiliation) and the Missouri Synod branch of the Lutheran Church in the United States. Quebe-

deaux also includes Campus Crusade for Christ, founded by
Bill Bright, in this category, and presumably (although he does
not mention it) Inter-Varsity.

The fourth stream Quebedeaux calls the new evangelicalism.
Carl Henry has discerned eight things which the young evangelicals expect from their churches:

1. An interest in human beings not simply as souls to be
saved, but as whole persons;

2. More active involvement by evangelical Christians in
socio-political affairs;

3. An honest look at many churches' idolatry of national-
ism;

4. Adoption of new forms of worship;

5. An end to judging spiritual commitment by such exter-
nals as dress, hair style, and other participation in cultural
trends, including rock music;

6. A new spirit with regard to ecumenical or nonecumenical
attitude;

7. Bold and, if need be, costly involvement in the revolu-
tionary struggles of our day; and finally,

8. A reappraisal of life values.[3]

Thus, American evangelicalism can be seen, from one aspect,
as following, roughly, the political spectrum from right to left.
The new evangelicalism challenges many assumptions that
evangelicals make, and seeks to strip away the cultural accre-
tions of the American way of life and thus expose the real gospel
of Jesus Christ and apply it accurately to every area of human
life. It questions the American dream. In a way it psychoana-
lyzes it—to distinguish between fact and fiction, reality and
falsehood.

To return to my own story, my earliest recollections of the
evangelicalism which burst upon me was of the second
stream—a reasonably open kind of fundamentalism. But it did
not satisfy me completely. I had too many pesky doubts about
its ultimate veracity. But I was soon to be in touch with
establishment evangelicalism or its nearest equivalent in Britain,
and there for the time being I found my complete satisfaction.

The person who I identified most clearly with was John Stott, whose ministry at All Souls, Langham Place, London, and his occasional visits to Cambridge University where I was a student seemed to epitomize for me what Christianity was chiefly about—a rational faith combined with intellectual integrity, and an openness to change, with a spirit of enquiry into basic presuppositions which had gone unchallenged for too long. I frankly wonder how long I would have remained an evangelical had I not come into close touch with the new evangelicalism which was arising in Britain at this time, and which was to owe so much to the ministry of John Stott at All Souls. The visit of Billy Graham to Britain in the 1950's and my six-year curacy at All Souls, Langham Place, were both powerful influences on my future.

In 1962 my charismatic experience meant I was to lose touch with the evangelical world for about twelve years. (Perhaps this is a good point at which to explain that I am not saying that *evangelical* and *charismatic* are necessarily mutually exclusive terms. That is, charismatics are not non-evangelicals as such, though for the purposes of this book I am referring to the two as distinct sisters in the Church.) But the trend in Britain in this period has been a continued polarization. As in the United States, ecumenism has been a chief catalyst. Some, identified largely with Dr. Martyn Lloyd-Jones, have swung to the right in totally repudiating the modern ecumenical movement and calling those who don't "guilty by association." Their chief organ has been *The Evangelical Times*, and their main strength has come from F.I.E.C. (Federation of Independent Evangelical Churches) and Baptist churches, with an emphasis on Calvinism. But others, chiefly Anglicans, led by men such as John Stott and Jim Packer, have swung to the left. They expressed themselves and their wholehearted commitment to their church and a wider ecumenism at the National Evangelical Anglican Congress at Keele in 1967.

There was also a commitment to responsible thought and action in the world—and the beginnings of a commitment to social action. Non-Anglicans have found the Evangelical Alliance the rallying-point for similar postures. The Evangelical Alliance has within its membership many Anglicans also, and John Stott was himself its president 1975-76. But the polarization has continued. In 1977, ten years after Keele, there was another N.E.A.C. conference, this time held at Nottingham, and all the evidence points in the direction of a continuation of the "new look" evangelicalism.

The same attitudes found expression at the 1974 Lausanne Congress on Evangelism. The Lausanne Covenant, for example, stated that "evangelism and socio-political involvement are *both* part of our Christian duty. For both are necessary expressions of our doctrines of God and man, our love for our neighbor and our obedience to Jesus Christ."[4]

THREE
THE PENTECOSTAL/ CHARISMATIC SCENE

Unfortunately it has to be recorded that evangelicalism has not been the best of friends with Pentecostals and charismatics. To begin with, Pentecostals were for the most part treated by evangelicals as heretics. Fortunately much of this is now past history. One hopes it is forgotten and forgiven, though the extreme fundamentalist camp still classifies Pentecostals and charismatics in the same category as Roman Catholics and modernists.

In 1976 the World Congress of Fundamentalists met in the Usher Hall in Edinburgh. The aim of the Congress was a "worldwide testimony to the inspiration, inerrancy, and authority of the Bible, exposing the unscriptural nature of 'new evangelicalism,' 'neoorthodoxy,' 'neo-pentecostalism,' the modern charismatic movement, and the cults and false religions which characterize the apostasy of our day." All were dismissed as "the devil's crowd." Speakers included Bob Jones and Ian Paisley. There was a Calvinist counterdemonstration at the Congress, and Dr. Carl McIntire refused to participate in the Congress.

But the more you move to the left in the evangelical world, the less opposition to charismatics you will find. In 1976 Fuller Seminary hired its first Pentecostal teacher—Dr. Russell Spitt-

23

ler. At the Lausanne Congress on Evangelism in 1974 several charismatics, including Juan Carlos Ortiz and Larry Christenson, were invited as participants. The same was true at the National Evangelical Anglican Congress at Nottingham in 1977, at which I was myself a contributor. And the Evangelical Alliance has had charismatic speakers such as David Pawson and David Watson at its conferences.

Many of the "young evangelicals" have either become actively involved in the charismatic renewal and have become some of its chief spokesmen, or have expressed both interest and support. It seems to relate to their more radical outlook, and to their search for personal, ecclesiastical, and social liberation. An evangelical scholar, Clark H. Pinnock, when on the staff of Regent College, Vancouver, Canada, wrote an article in *Christianity Today* entitled "The New Pentecostalism— Reflection by a Well-wisher." It epitomized the new outlook that many evangelicals have toward Pentecostalism. He wrote, "The new Pentecostal movement seems to this observer to be a genuine movement of the Spirit of God renewing his Church. I speak as an observer who, though standing outside the new Pentecostalism proper, has learned to appreciate it from personal involvement in charismatic groups, both Protestant and Catholic. From these experiences I have emerged a stronger and better Christian. I agree with Karl Barth that there may often be too little of the pneumatic in the Church, but never too much. Therefore, it thrills my soul to see multitudes of people allowing the Spirit to operate freely in their midst."[5]

Having looked at evangelicalism, let us now turn to the charismatic world today. It is necessary for clarity to distinguish between the Pentecostal churches and those involved in the historic churches who claim a "Pentecostal experience." So we shall refer to the former as Pentecostals and the latter as charismatics.

As we have already seen, it is difficult enough to describe the evangelical world with any precision. Evangelicals can be as divided among themselves as they are separate from other streams of the Church. But it is even harder to delineate the various strata of Pentecostal spirituality. Professor Walter Hollenweger has demonstrated this in his *magnum opus The Pentecostals*.[6] But even he has not been able to cope with the modern kaleidoscope called "Pentecostalism." Many people have drawn attention to its divisive tendencies. But all too often the implication has been that this has been of a cancerous nature. Pentecostals have been often accused of malignant sectarianism. This is unfair.

In some ways their abilities to adapt to different environments and cultures is to be commended rather than censured. Those who are looking for drab uniformity may well be unimpressed. But God's Holy Spirit is never dull in his outworkings, and what to us may constitute a surprise may say more about our prejudices and cultural predilections than the truth of the matter. That is not to say that Pentecostals have not been guilty of individualism and shortsighted policies in relationship to their own movement. But the general impression one gets is that many, especially evangelicals, are quick to give blanket disapproval of Pentecostalism on the basis of cultural rather than rational or scriptural arguments.

Pentecostals are evangelicals at heart. Both of the leading Pentecostal denominations in Britain (Assemblies of God and Elim) are members of the Evangelical Alliance. This body has quietly sought to reconcile Pentecostals to their fellow evangelicals, who have traditionally regarded them with the utmost caution and suspicion. It has also for many years shown interest in the charismatic movement, while the Church of England Evangelical Council (chaired by the Rev. John R. W. Stott) had until 1974 largely ignored it.

J. Edwin Orr has said that if you scratch a Pentecostal, you will find an Arminian. This is basically true. Pentecostalism grew out of the tradition of Wesleyan Arminianism rather than the Calvinism associated with Wesley's contemporary, George Whitefield. There have been some notable exceptions to this, particularly the late Pastor Billy Richards of Slough, England, who until his death was one of the most outstanding Assemblies of God pastors.

Pentecostals can, therefore, be found in the four streams of the evangelical world previously discussed. Some are strict fundamentalists, with a passionate dislike of Rome and the World Council of Churches and a literalistic attitude to the Scriptures. In their relationship with evangelical fundamentalists, they are inclined toward as much distrust as they receive, and there is no love lost between the two. But younger Pentecostals often have a different attitude toward the historic churches, and there is a small but significant ground swell of new biblical studies. This may suggest that some Pentecostals are forsaking many of the assumptions of their forefathers with regard to the doctrines of the Church and prophecy, and even with regard to the Holy Spirit and *charismata*.

In addition, there are now a significant number of Pentecostals who have broken away from the straitjacket of their Pentecostal denominations, run up the charismatic flag, and incurred the displeasure and ostracism of their peers. Notable among these is the Rev. Ralph Wilkerson, pastor of the huge Melodyland complex in Anaheim, California.

Some in the Pentecostal movement have not yet come to terms with the charismatic movement. They still eye it with suspicion and distrust. They do not know how to behave toward it, whether to treat it as a rival or a friend. Some Pentecostals regard it as a counterfeit, some kind of Frankenstein monster—Pentecostalism gone wrong. At successive World Conferences of the Pentecostal movement, the charismatic movement has been largely ignored. Much work needs to be done to overcome these barriers of misapprehension.

Pentecostalism was born in the ferment of fierce controversy. Their leaders became convinced that the churches would never listen to their message or want to share their experience of the Holy Spirit. It has been hard for them to accept the reality or the sincerity of those now within the churches who, while claiming to share their experience of charismatic Christianity, have elected to remain within their denominations rather than join the fellowship of Pentecostal churches.

Pentecostals have felt hurt that charismatics have largely

ignored them. It has been difficult for them to accept the new attitude of denominational leaders and others toward charismatic experience. They have been tempted to believe that the only real answer is that charismatics have compromised and "undersold" the message. If they had the real thing and preached the "full gospel," they too would have been thrown out of the churches. Pentecostals have waited in vain for this to happen, but it hasn't, much to their chagrin. All this is understandable. But as Pentecostalism matures and the old theological wounds are healed, progress is being made. A new generation of Pentecostals is coming to the fore, who have never experienced the kind of bitterness that was so common in the early days.

But we must now turn to the charismatic movement itself. Until comparatively recently it has seemed to present a united front. But discerning observers would have noticed for some years rifts developing which have become more noticeable in recent years. Like most new movements, it began with practically no organization or structure. It has developed in a piece-meal fashion, and the American influence has ensured its basically pragmatic approach.

For a good many years there were few organizations in the United States capable of giving any direction to the renewal, or even wanting to. Most of the early influence came either from the Full Gospel Businessmen's Fellowship International (FGBMFI); or from charismatic churches such as Melodyland, St. Luke's (Seattle), or the Church of the Redeemer (Houston); or from the advent of charismatic conferences such as The Pittsburgh Charismatic Conference, started in 1969; or from the growing number of charismatic speakers who circulated around the country with the same kind of enthusiasm as Wesley's itinerant preachers, and with much the same kind of response and success. Charismatic books have been a great influence also.

But by the 1970's new influences began to be felt. The birth of the Roman Catholic charismatic renewal or Catholic Pentecostalism in 1967 was small and largely unheralded. But within

27

a very short time it was to be the dominant force in the charismatic movement, wielding an influence throughout the whole world, though chiefly and significantly in the United States. Roman Catholic charismatics began to do what Episcopal and Protestant charismatics had largely failed to do—they started organizing themselves.

Before long, communities were being formed, initially inspired by the example and experience of the Episcopal Church of the Redeemer, Houston. A leadership became established. Some were recognized leaders, others were not. It became apparent that the future was not going to be a vague free-for-all, but a well-organized movement. We shall be discussing some of the problems which this attitude has raised later; but for the moment we need to see the change that all this brought to the charismatic movement, altering its emphasis and ultimately its general direction.

Other churches were not slow to follow the Roman Catholic lead. Although there had been some attempts before to organize charismatic groups within denominations, the Roman Catholics gave new and incisive impetus to this, and there sprang up the Episcopal Charismatic Fellowship, the Presbyterian Charismatic Communion, etc. The Roman Catholics were soon organizing an annual National Conference, held for a number of years now on the campus of Notre Dame University, South Bend, Indiana. This has grown dramatically, with attendance topping the 30,000 mark at recent conferences. Others followed their lead.

The old chorus which was sung so vociferously at the FGBMFI banquets in American cities from coast to coast—"I don't care what church you belong to"—was quietly dropped from the charismatic repertoire. A Catholic song took over in popularity—"We are one in the Spirit . . . and we pray that all unity may one day be restored . . ." The Roman Catholic contribution was both dramatic and decisive. Denominational Christianity was back in fashion, at least for the time being.

While the Roman Catholics were organizing themselves in their twin centers of South Bend, Indiana, and Ann Arbor,

Michigan, something else was happening in the South which was to have considerable influence in the seventies. A few charismatic teachers got together and founded the Holy Spirit Teaching Mission in Fort Lauderdale, Florida. (Later the name was to be changed to Christian Growth Ministries.) At first sight there was as little in common between these two groups as there is between the climate and politics of Florida and Indiana or Michigan. The Roman Catholic groups were led by intellectual laymen whose politics reflected somewhat the liberalism of the Kennedys. The Fort Lauderdale set-up was led by pastors from evangelical or Pentecostal churches whose politics were much more reminiscent of Barry Goldwater. The Roman Catholics would normally have looked askance at the biblical fundamentalism of men like Derek Prince, Charles Simpson, and Bob Mumford, while the Fort Lauderdale men would have been deeply suspicious of anything coming from Roman Catholicism. Yet the mutuality of these two camps in the 1970's was to be a moment of great significance, which was bound to have a profound influence on the future of the charismatic movement.

During the 1960's the front-runner in the United States was undoubtedly the FGBMFI. If you read the testimony literature of those years, one of the constantly recurring influences was this remarkable organization. But the birth of the Roman Catholic movement owed more initially to classical Pentecostalism than it did to the more "secular" approach of the Full Gospel Businessmen. It was "secular" in the sense that it owed a great deal of its initial success to the fact that its policy was always to meet in hotels or secular institutions rather than on church premises. Thus it demonstrated a neutral stance in ecclesiastical affairs. It also sidestepped the numerous doctrinal issues that were already percolating by having a plethora of personal testimonies rather than Bible teaching. If speakers attempted to change this pattern, they were "testimonied" out.

But the Holy Spirit Teaching Mission, while sharing some of the approach of the FGBMFI, differed greatly, as their name implies, from that organization's policy regarding teaching.

They faced controversial issues squarely, made up their own minds what was true, and then taught it to Christians by every possible means. Thus, the Fort Lauderdale leaders acted for many years like a major fault beneath the earth's surface, periodically sending seismic shock waves through the charismatic movement.

Water baptism was one of the first tremors to be felt. Photos of ecstatic immersions off Florida beaches were published in their literature. Next was the exorcism earthquake. Derek Prince and Don Basham spread the deliverance ministry throughout North America. But the greatest shake-up of all was to come in 1975. I am referring to the discipleship controversy. (See page 91 for a fuller description of this issue and Appendix C, page 139 for an official report on how the issue was resolved.)

Without at this point going into the details of those controversies, the point to notice is that Christian Growth Ministries (originally the Holy Spirit Teaching Mission), although at the beginning poles apart from the Roman Catholics, was in fact doing the same kind of thing—organizing charismatics, teaching them, facing Christian issues, and seeking to balance the excessive emphasis on testimony. The fact that the teaching was based on a literalistic interpretation of the Scriptures is not of importance at this point.

The thing that is important is that a few gifted men, supported by a small but influential body of lay people and armed with the skillful and sophisticated use of the media, had by the mid-1970's secured one of the strongest positions in the charismatic movement in the United States. If the discipleship issue had not come up, they would have had the support of a large number of charismatic leaders and organizations in America.

By the time the discipleship issue broke on the American scene, the Roman Catholic and Fort Lauderdale leaders had already been fraternizing for some time. The issue drew them closer together as they found common ground in their emphasis on submission and authority in the Church, and their interest in para-church structures rather than the renewal of the institutional Church itself. Also, the Roman Catholic renewal has from its inception tended to be more "Pentecostal" in its style of worship—as has the Fort Lauderdale group. Here again was common ground. But not all charismatics have been prepared to follow this particular lead.

The principles of discipleship they stressed cut across the grain of some basic patterns of the American way of life. They challenged its individualism, the American's right to do his own thing. Americans are naturally suspicious of any interference with their private lives and the rights of the individual. Their discipleship smelled dangerously like Christian socialism. Organizations such as the FGBMFI and churches like Melodyland were sharply critical of Christians taking authority over other Christians, and of the principle that *all* Christians should be submitted to someone else. It was panic stations for some as if their very life depended upon it.

Kathryn Kuhlman uncharacteristically jumped in with both feet. After many years of studiously avoiding controversial issues within the body of Christ (she had herself more than her ration of controversy), she condemned the "disciplers" and warned people about their teaching. Since Kathryn Kuhlman's death a number of biographies have been published, giving more of an insight into the life and career of this turbulent personality. Knowing what we now know about her, it is understandable that she reacted as she did, for the teaching about submission was pretty near the bone for a woman who had submitted to no one during her life after her mother had beaten the living daylights out of her as a child.

But apart from the more emotional reactions of charismatic groups and personalities there were many others who, while accepting some of the new teaching, were not prepared to take the whole of it and saw certain dangers in the new emphasis coming from Fort Lauderdale and the Ann Arbor-South Bend axis. Not all Roman Catholics in any case are closely identified with the Ann Arbor and South Bend leadership. Edward O'Connor, for example, who was one of the founders of the renewal in the University of Notre Dame, resigned early in the 1970's from his leadership role, while continuing to work and teach within the charismatic renewal. In 1976 a new magazine called *Catholic Charismatics* was launched by Paulist Press to cater to Catholics of this kind and to give expression to emphases rather different from those of Ann Arbor and South Bend.

But when we leave the shores of the New World we find a very different situation from that in the United States, a situation which Americans sometimes find hard both to understand and to appreciate. The charismatic renewal outside the United States is principally to be found within existing churches, *not* in para-church structures. It is true there are groups and organizations which approximate to the Church Growth Ministries of Fort Lauderdale, and there are covenant communities which are associated with the American Catholic approach. These have accepted the discipleship principles more or less.

An example of this influence is the work of Brian Smith and others in Brisbane, Australia. A number of covenant communities have been set up, which owe much to the Ann Arbor community, which they would regard as a kind of "mother house." But by no means are all Roman Catholic charismatics in Australia following this particular line.

The influence of the Fountain Trust in Britain has been quite different from the American approach. The Trust from its inception eschewed para-church developments. It declared itself "for the Church," and committed to the costly ministry of being a prophetic voice *within* the Church. It has, therefore, actively discouraged the formation of groups other than for temporary purposes, and instead committed itself to local church renewal for better or for worse.

The results speak for themselves. Although in some ways there is less to show for the renewal "on the ground," the solid heart of the movement is to be found in the growing number of Anglican, Baptist, Methodist, and other churches which are being changed by the Holy Spirit from the inside out. In contrast to the largely pessimistic attitude of American charismatics to institutional Christianity in general and denominational churches in particular—the popularly held opinion that "the churches are finished"—the Fountain Trust, while not denying the need for radical change, has expressed its faith in the Church and its ability to be renewed by the Spirit. It has stood firmly for the principle of staying within one's church, and not leaving it to form new charismatic churches, however attractive a proposition this may seem to be.

The Fountain Trust's approach has influenced the renewal in other countries, and organizations such as the Temple Trust in Australia and Christian Advance Ministries in New Zealand have largely modeled themselves on it. In these two countries, even more strikingly than in Britain, the renewal is to be seen mainly in the local church, and not in new structures.

There is hardly a single Roman Catholic church throughout the world that has been renewed by the Holy Spirit. But it is not that the Catholic charismatic renewal has failed to bring this about. It is truer to say it has never really regarded this as its main objective. Its main purpose has been to set up an alternative church society, with a very loose connection to the institutional church and its hierarchy, and so be free to do and be what it believes the Lord wants of it.

Christian Growth Ministries in Fort Lauderdale had similar objectives. Its leaders were not associated closely with denominations. It encouraged new churches as well as the renewal of the old, while at the same time not opposing the churches, but fellowshiping as much as possible with them.

We have mentioned some of the similarities between evangelicals and Pentecostals and charismatics. All turn to the Bible for their final authority. All believe in "supernatural" Christianity, even if there may be differences as to the extent to which the power and gifts of the Holy Spirit are available today. All are committed to evangelism and world mission.

But there are differences. The charismatic movement, for example, is more ecumenical than the evangelical world. The evangelical tends to define his frontiers more definitely and

33

guard them more jealously. The charismatic movement is still amorphous, even if recent attempts have been made to structure it more definitely. It is more difficult to label a charismatic than it is an evangelical. Charismatic Christianity has flowed into all sections of the Church and had its influence on Catholics and liberals alike. It would be impossible for charismatics as a body to define their doctrines, because of the great variety expressed. What basically unites charismatics is not doctrine, but experience.

Although this may be controverted by some, I feel the charismatic movement is more closely in touch with the "grass-roots" than evangelicals are. Not only do they compass a wider social range, but their leaders are in better touch with their constituents than evangelicals tend to be. There is more empathy between leaders and the led. The leadership tends to reflect more rank-and-file opinion. It seems to be more a movement "of the people and for the people" than the evangelical world, and this accounts in part for its worldwide appeal and its rapid growth in recent years. It is still a popular movement, capable of gathering large crowds of people to hear leaders who will receive popular acclaim because they are saying roughly what those listening want to hear and want to hear often. Thus, clapping and cheering have become a part of many charismatic gatherings, although there are cultural aspects to this, particularly the influence of Roman Catholics.

The charismatic movement is still much smaller numerically than evangelicalism. But although it is not as strong in influence, it covers a much wider cross section of the Church and, therefore, has a unique function as a bridge-builder. Because it has penetrated the Roman Catholic and Protestant worlds to about the same extent, it has bridge-building potential of importance to the ecumenical future of the Church.

FOUR
THE ROMAN
CATHOLIC SCENE

For some it may be a hard enough thing to think of a partner-ship between evangelicals and charismatics. But many would say that to bring Roman Catholics in for good measure is going too far. As in Cornelius Ryan's war story, it is "a bridge too far." One bridge is possible, but to try to bridge the Catholic/Protestant chasm at the same time is to attempt the impossible. Many would say that it would be decidedly undiplomatic to try; it might well scuttle a possible drawing together of evangelicals and charismatics. Not only do most Pentecostals regard the Roman Catholic Church with the utmost suspicion; but there are also at least some charismatics who are hesitant about them, and most evangelicals keep away from these whom they still regard as heretics.

An easy answer might be, "If this be so, the Holy Spirit seems to have shown himself to be singularly undiplomatic." From the moment in 1967 when the first Roman Catholics began to experience charismatic renewal, it has very largely been an ecumenical adventure for them. It is not without significance that Ireland has pioneered the new charismatic ecumenism, insisting from the inception of the movement that the annual National Conference be, among other things, a witness to love between churches in a land torn with sectarian violence.

In 1977 other countries followed suit. In January Protestants and Catholics shared a joint charismatic conference in Sydney, Australia. In July, Roman Catholics in the United States canceled their own conference in order to meet with many non-Catholics in a giant conference in Kansas City. The Fountain Trust conference held in Guildford, England, in 1971 was for the first time shared by Catholics and non-Catholics. The disasters predicted by some have not taken place. Rather, the movement has grown and deepened as a result of this cross-fertilization.

David Watson comments on this in *Crusade* magazine: "I can see that the Holy Spirit is strengthening in different traditions and denominations those areas which are weak. Evangelicals have rediscovered the work of the Holy Spirit, the importance of worship and the Church as the body of Christ; the Roman Catholics have rediscovered the Bible, conversion and evangelism."[7] The Rector of one of Britain's liveliest evangelical churches (St. Michael-le-Belfrey, York) sums it up: "In many ways, I feel the charismatic renewal is God's own sort of ecumenical movement."

Watson confesses that like many evangelicals, he was fearful of his first real encounter with Roman Catholics in the flesh. It took place at the Fountain Trust 1971 Guildford conference. He writes about it: "I tried to find out what these men really believed about the crucial issues such as the authority of Scripture, justification by faith, the Virgin Mary. I was fearful lest our unity be based only on experience and not on truth. When we'd cleared away a lot of semantics, I could not see any essential difference between what they believe and what I believed. On basics we were one in Christ though there might be some differences of opinion on secondary issues."

Granted, some official Roman Catholic doctrines refuse to line up with clear biblical teaching. But does this bury the possibility of genuine Christian fellowship between Catholic and non-Catholic believers in Christ? Watson thinks not, and I agree.

There is every indication that the charismatic movement has

been a kind of incubator helping to hatch all kinds of new and exciting things. But one wonders how fertile all this would have been had not Roman Catholics, charismatics, and evangelicals worshiped, worked, and shared together through these years.

It is as difficult as ever to describe accurately the Roman Catholic Church today. There are the extremes, as in every church. On the conservative wing we have the "Affaire Lefebvre." Archbishop Marcel Lefebvre has defied the Pope and heads a small but vociferous minority who are bent on overthrowing some aspects of Vatican II, and especially in restoring the Tridentine Mass. It is alleged that his movement, which is strongly anticommunist, is financed by right-wing industrialists in northern France and the United States. Accusing his Church of betraying principles to the Protestants, the Archbishop commands very little support among most Catholics, who remain loyal both to the Pope and to the spirit, if not the letter, of Vatican II.

On the other wing there are those Catholics in South America, for example, who are openly Marxist and who preach the theology of liberation. Others, though not sharing the extreme left-wing political aspirations of some, are openly modern and extremely liberal in their theological predilections.

Pluralism is definitely in vogue in the Roman Catholic Church today; there is no longer any authoritative constraint. The boundaries have become vague and indefinite. Few are quite sure where they are, and those who claim to be sure cannot agree among themselves exactly where their certainties lie. Seldom has the Roman Catholic Church gone through such a time of confusion. The mists of uncertainty seem to have descended on the Vatican. Some are deeply troubled. Bill McSweeney wrote in the British newspaper The Times of a Church "that opposes nothing; that for fear of giving offence, always sits down to be counted."[8]

The Roman Catholic charismatic movement has emerged from neither extreme, although (especially in South America) it has definite leftist leanings. It owes much to a handful of resolute laymen who put their faith to work adventurously and

37

won the day when few would have given them much chance. Kevin Ranaghan in South Bend and Ralph Martin with a number of able lieutenants seemed to have from the very beginning a deft touch in steering the renewal through some pretty tricky waters. It has been able to maintain an enthusiastic Pentecostal surge, while avoiding the worse features of fanaticism or a limp scholasticism. It was kept in tune with many of the vibrating chords of the American religious tradition, and so from the beginning has always been a popular movement.

At the same time, it has gone out of its way to keep in range of the hierarchy, and to seek its approval wherever possible. At least judging by its results, the movement has been an encouragement to Catholic leaders who had more or less resigned themselves to the discouraging statistics of a large-scale religious recession. A new vibrant Catholicism seems to be arising phoenix-like from the ashes of the Post-Vatican II darkness and depression.

The accession of Cardinal Suenens to the movement in the early 1970's contributed further to the mounting prestige of the Catholic charismatic renewal. One of the most influential men in the world's largest Church, Cardinal Suenens' unusual blend of conservatism and radical liberalism was exactly what was needed. For the movement is innately conservative in its loyalty to Catholic tradition and its submission to lawful authority, while at the same time being radical in its approach to liturgy, evangelism, and community.

The Roman Catholic Church has long had the reputation of being able to handle hot potatoes with amazing deftness. The word "panic" is not part of its vocabulary. Catholics take their time and weigh situations with considerable care. They know how easy it is to throw the baby out with the bathwater; and that in the final analysis, it is better to keep both than to lose both. So they have kept the baby and the bathwater.

The reaction of the Roman Catholic bishops in the United States to the renewal is now famous. They encouraged and warned, and set up liaison personnel to keep the movement in touch with the Church. Their policy has been to keep their reins on the movement, but to hold them very lightly. If the horse bolts, they can do something about it. But for the meantime, let it find its own way. The rider trusts that the horse has some sense and knows what it's doing.

This has been in marked contrast to some evangelical leaders who, to continue the analogy, have either pulled the reins in tightly or in desperation shot the poor horse dead. There is little doubt that the traditional open attitude of the Roman Catholic Church to movements of all sorts has been an important factor in the development of the Catholic charismatic renewal.

FIVE
IS SUCH A
UNITY
POSSIBLE?

It is my own conviction that a growing unity between the three
forces in the Christian world is both desirable and possible.
After five years' participation in dialogue with Roman Catholics and several years with evangelicals, I have formed the con-
clusion that the things which unite us are both more numerous
and more weighty than the things which divide us. The Holy
Spirit is so obviously at work in all three worlds that only good
can come from an increasing unity, which need not be thought
to compromise the essential convictions of those involved.

We need to recognize that there is always a danger of a false
and superficial unity which can be a betrayal of truth for the
sake of expediency. But this must always be weighed against the
opposite danger, the weakness that prevails when Christians are
not together, and the besmirching of the name of Jesus Christ
which our divisions inevitably incite. Immense advantages
would accrue if these three influential forces were to flow
together. It is difficult, for example, to see how God's
evangelistic program for the world can be fulfilled without the
Roman Catholic Church, whose influence in terms of man-
power resources in countries like France, Italy, the South
American nations, Mexico, and India far exceed anything that
Protestants can put forward.

On the other hand, these resources need to be renewed by the Holy Spirit and released if they are going to make the impact they potentially have. And for this they need both the inspiration of the evangelical and charismatic movements. But it is by no means a one-way system. All three forces in the Body of Christ need each other. Evangelicalism needs to be delivered from its excessive individualism and its innate conservatism. It needs to discover for itself the meaning of community. The charismatic movement left on its own would almost certainly become another denomination. It needs to be part of something larger than itself. It needs to have its own particular insights balanced by those of others.

But there are at least three major foundations upon which such a unity can be built.

The first is *a common respect for the Bible and the fundamentals of the faith*. Evangelicals, charismatics, and Roman Catholics regard the Bible as the authoritative basis of Christian truth. Opinions may vary regarding interpretation of passages and principles of hermeneutics. Some will emphasize one part, which another may tend to neglect. Some will be fundamentalist, interpreting the Bible literally. Some will believe *only* what is contained in Scripture. Others will believe anything provided it is not contrary to Scripture. But all three believe in the essential foundations or fundamentals of Christian doctrine: the Virgin Birth, the Atonement of Christ for our sins, the deity of Christ, the empty tomb, the gift of the Holy Spirit at Pentecost, and the return of Christ.

The second is *a common concern for evangelism and world mission*. All three are thoroughly committed to personal evangelism, with the conviction that since salvation comes from Christ alone, every person needs to come to Christ if he is to be saved and become part of Christ's Body the Church. Although Roman Catholics often see this in sacramental terms, bringing candidates to baptism, there is much evidence that on the continent of Europe and on the mission fields of the world, Roman Catholics see adult baptism as more normal, and see the need to bring each person to a definite commitment to the

Lordship of Christ and faith in his name. This is especially true when Roman Catholics become involved in the charismatic movement. A personal faith in Jesus Christ is regarded by Catholic charismatics as an essential prerequisite for the experience of the baptism in the Holy Spirit.

Thus Cardinal Suenens writes words which have been echoed thousands of times by evangelical evangelists: "To be a true Christian means to have met Jesus personally as Savior and as Lord. I must accept Jesus totally, as a reality, the Lord and Master of my life as I live and experience it day by day."[9] The Cardinal goes on to speak of this "as a gradual process, not the work of a day." Evangelicals might disagree (although a growing number would have to admit that for many, "conversion" is not as clearcut as some have emphasized, that the norm is usually a kind of "growing into" faith, rather than a once-for-all split-second decision of a lifetime). But there is far more ground for agreement than there might have been thought possible a few years ago.

"A Christian is a changed person," Cardinal Suenens writes, "a convert; he has turned away from himself, so as to adhere to Jesus of Nazareth who, for his sake, died and rose from the dead. He has made a personal discovery of Jesus, and acknowledged him as the Christ, the unique Son of the Father, the Anointed One of the Holy Spirit." Of course, the Cardinal is not speaking for all Roman Catholics. But he would be expressing the convictions of a significant number, and it is clear that such evangelical statements are in keeping with the doctrinal position of the Church at large.

The *ex opere operato* concept as it relates to baptism is *not* the declaration of a purely magical action in the sacrament, for it refers to the one who performs the sacrament rather than the person being baptized. A closer look at Roman Catholic sacramental teaching reveals that St. Thomas Aquinas' opinion was that "without faith nothing happens."

One wishes one could also say that the three forces share a common concern for social action. We have already pointed out how divided the evangelical world is on this particular issue. The same could be said of both the charismatic and Roman Catholic camps. Nevertheless, it can truthfully be said that there is a noticeable ground swell in all three. The Lausanne Congress on Evangelism, through the *Lausanne Covenant*, committed the largest and most influential section of the evangelical world to social action. The wording was this: "Although reconciliation with man is not reconciliation with God, nor is social action evangelism, nor is political liberation salvation, nevertheless we affirm that evangelism and sociopolitical involvement are both part of our Christian duty. For both are necessary expressions of our doctrines of God and man, our love for our neighbor, and our obedience to Jesus Christ."[10] It concludes with the words of Scripture, "Faith without works is dead."

At the same time, the trend in the Roman Catholic Church since Vatican II has been toward a genuine commitment to the world and its needs. While not many might subscribe to the extreme position of the "Theology of Liberation" school of thought, led by Gustavo Gutierrez, a growing number of Roman Catholics would want to see their Church associated with every effort to bring social and economic justice to the world. The charismatic movement too has been influenced by the Roman Catholics since they "joined" it in 1967. The FGBMFI and Fort Lauderdale conservative bias has been more than counteracted. Many were gratified to see that the new charismatic newspaper *The National Courier*[11] reflected in its editorial policy liberal political ideologies rather than the more traditional conservative attitudes of Pentecostals and fundamentalists.

The third foundation of unity is *a common belief in the supernatural*. All three have reacted in varying degrees to the influences of modernism, with its almost wholesale rejection of the supernatural in the experience of modern man, and its attempts both to demythologize the Scriptures and to reinterpret Jesus Christ in more "natural" terms.

One of the main planks of the evangelical message is that man is by nature a child of the devil, and therefore only a supernatural new-birth experience through faith in Jesus Christ can "save" him. Evangelical "miracles" are normally restricted to the new birth. Traditionally evangelicals have been skeptical both of the claims of Pentecostals and charismatics to spiritual gifts and miracles (including healing), and of Roman Catholic claims regarding sacramental "miracles," especially at baptism and in the eucharist. Roman Catholics have not had the same problems regarding miracles beyond sacramental grace. A Church that can so wholeheartedly support a center like Lourdes, whatever one may say about the miracles associated with it, obviously is open to the miraculous in our day.

With the evangelical world thoroughly penetrated by charismatic experience, there are fewer now who would still subscribe to a dispensationalism that relegates spiritual gifts and miracles to the first century. Few now agree with the expressed views of B. B. Warfield, whose influence on evangelicalism in the first half of the twentieth century was profound—that the supernatural gifts were so wholly associated with the apostles that when they had all died, the gifts were buried with them. Likewise, fewer Christians now assume certain spiritual gifts to have ended when the New Testament was completed.

So we see in all three camps a faith in the supernatural breaking out from the narrow confines of biblical fundamentalism, mechanical sacramentalism, and traditional dispensationalism. The ghosts of Scofield and Warfield are in some sense being laid to rest.

WHO IS LEFT OUT?

It is fairly obvious that not all would be happy with such a partnership. In fact, some would strenuously deny that such a moving together would be in the best interest of the one Holy Catholic and Apostolic Church. The extreme right wing of the evangelical world would fulminate against it, since they link together Roman Catholics, modernists, and charismatics as false prophets and heretics. They would regard such an alliance as wholly evil and a betrayal of the truth.

Equally, the extreme right wing of the Roman Catholic world, the traditionalists, would see in such an alliance further damning evidence of the trend of the Roman Catholic Church toward becoming more Protestant. Not all charismatics would applaud such a unity either. It too has a right wing, and many independents, especially those who come from the Fort Lauderdale-independent-church sphere of influence, seem to be looking for another kind of unity, a kind of charismatic united nations, people drawn from the various churches to form God's end-time army which is to prepare the way for the return of the King.

There are also whole sections of people with more moderate opinions, who do not identify easily with any of these three camps. There are those who have been mostly influenced by liberal theology, who cannot accept some (if any) of the fundamentals of the faith, and who do not see the need for a supernatural change in a man's life for him to become a Christian. There is a whole section who would perhaps call themselves Christian humanists, who do not have either a pessimistic attitude toward human nature, nor the idea of man's inevitable progress, nor confidence in a God who dramatically and faithfully intervenes in the affairs of man.

Then there is the World Council of Churches and its considerable influence within the churches. It has so far failed in its attempts to woo the Roman Catholic Church, which has refused to join their ecumenical club. It has until recently ignored the charismatic movement, except where it has some socio-political interests to share, as for example the West Indian Pentecostals in Britain, who have shown themselves more politically alive than white Pentecostals and more articulately socialist in political persuasion.

But these attitudes are changing. Largely at first under the leadership of Canon Rex Davis, and now through his successor at its Geneva headquarters, David Gill, the WCC is both researching and making positive contacts with the charismatic movement all over the world. In September 1977, the first consultation was held at Rostrevor, Co. Down in Northern

Ireland, at which I was myself present. Further meetings are intended in the coming years.

If one is right in stressing that the ecumenical future lies in the direction of the coming together of these three influential forces in Christendom, then such a coming together needs to be open to these other elements, however strongly opposed or however indifferent they may be to the "sisters" we have described. We all ultimately belong together, and our bridges need to be kept intact and our contacts maintained with conservative right-wingers as well as politically active left-wingers. Dialogue needs to continue wherever those who profess to be Christians are divided from each other. Elitism is not a Christian characteristic, and any growth in Christian unity needs to be thankfully, but *humbly* accepted. We must not make it harder for others who see things differently to come together with us and us with them for that greater unity for which Christ died and for which the Holy Spirit was poured out.

THE THREE SISTERS SUMMARIZED

Of course, the three sisters have this in common: they all have the same Father. We are capable of painting the most grotesque caricatures of each of them. We can play duckpins with them and bowl them over with the greatest of ease by simply placing the best features of one against the worst of another.

At the same time it is almost impossible to arrive at the average evangelical or the average charismatic or the average Catholic. Each of the sisters possesses a veritable kaleidoscope of characteristics. But if we are charitable (and ought we not to be as Christians?), and look for the best in each, we shall begin to see how important it is that these sisters begin to move together. They need each other. Each is indispensable to the other.

We need to forgive what is bad in each, as indeed we need to be forgiven by others for the bad which is in us. Our happiest memories of each should make us want to see ourselves together rather than separate, and make us feel that a part of us now belongs to each. My evangelical part has indelibly printed on it a love for the Scriptures. I owe this to my evangelical heritage. Also, I still feel deeply the concern for preaching the gospel and bringing others to Christ, which is another of the hallmarks of the evangelical faith. Upon these two pillars I still build my life, and though there are now some other pillars, these two remain. And let it be added, the new pillars tone in very effectively with the old.

My charismatic part is different. Renewal for me has above all else given me a sense of delight I never possessed before, especially in worship. I have begun to recover what A. W. Tozer called "the missing jewel." It isn't only that worship has a priority it never had before. The quality and nature of worship has also changed for me. The cork has come out of the bottle. Worship is now for me a free and spontaneous expression of God's love in my heart.

Faith too has acquired a new dimension. Whereas evangelical faith gave me a quiet and restful confidence in the historical actions of Christ, which was indeed (as far as it went) liberating and deeply satisfying, charismatic faith has given me a new confidence in an ever present Lord who can, and often wishes to, intervene simply and sometimes dramatically in our daily lives. Everything that happens—from newspaper stories, the morning mail, telephone conversations, the routine decisions of life—are signs of God's love and care and are opportunities to see him actively at work in our human situation. Lost keys, broken down cars, aches and pains, financial crises, as well as the things that go right for us, are fascinating opportunities of proving the faithfulness of God in everything.

For many, the Holy Spirit seems to catch us slightly off-balance, and while we are sent sprawling we almost accidentally discover a new dimension of love which was not there before. Because our eyes are turned (by the Spirit, who specializes in this particular way of working) from the old labels we were once familiar with, to our Lord himself, we find ourselves loving people and accepting them, when before we ignored or spurned them. What I have since discovered really happened was that the Holy Spirit dealt a blow at the colossus of fear in me which had kept people conveniently at arm's length, and showed me that God's love cannot coexist with that fear. One or the other has to go. And when love exorcises fear, we find ourselves closer to certain kinds of people than was possible before.

It is rather more difficult to diagnose and describe the Catholic part of me. I was almost totally ignorant of everything Pentecostal or charismatic before finding myself launched into that brave new world. In many ways there were few fears or misunderstandings, because there was so little knowledge or understanding to misunderstand. But with the Catholic scene it was totally different. I had studied Roman Catholicism. I had assiduously read anti-Catholic literature. I had well-formulated prejudices and fears. Although I was never a fanatical anti-papist, I could see little that I liked about anything Catholic, and most of it I disliked intensely. I regarded Catholicism as confusing and a force which was actively working against the spread of the true evangelical faith. Catholics were my self-appointed enemies. If I ever met any "nice" Catholics (on reflection, most Catholics I met were in this category), I re-garded their "niceness" as a deceptive veneer. They were really wolves in sheep's clothing and I wasn't going to be taken in.

So when my prejudices melted and I found myself increasingly meeting and sharing with Roman Catholics, I seldom encountered them without a frog in my throat and a watering in my eyes. I now loved those whom I had previously rejected. Only when such personal prejudices are removed are we free to see Christ in our brothers. Then the Holy Spirit is able to teach us what he wants to through them. Oh, what an enrichment it has been to meet with Catholics and to be introduced to some of the treasure stores of Catholic life! The Virgin Mary has come alive and I feel I know her now, in the same way as my evangelical heritage helped me to know St. Paul. I have come to love God's creation and the gifts of creativity he has given to his people. Nature and nature's art have come alive. Above all, I have come to love the Church and its historical heritage. For the first time I have seen something of the richness of the Church before the Reformation. The sacraments have come alive too. Not as lifeless mechanical rites, but as "effectual signs," to use the language of the Reformers, or signs that work when there is faith. Holy Communion is for me like an oasis in a parched desert.

So we have met Evangeline, Charisma, and Roma—the three sisters. But does that complete the family? I know there is at least one more sister that I have never really met. I have sometimes seen her in the distance. I understand her name is Orthodoxa. Somehow the rest of the family seems incomplete without her. I must confess I have neither avoided her, nor made strenuous efforts to meet her and get to know her. Our paths have very seldom crossed. I have been so taken up with cultivating my friendship with the other three sisters that I have had little time left over to give to this other sister. But this book is sadly incomplete without her.

Maybe the next big movement of the Holy Spirit will be the enrichment of our family life with the inclusion in close friendship of Orthodoxa—and this sister's own enrichment also in sharing openly with her other sisters. For there is "one body and one Spirit . . . one Lord, one faith, one baptism, one God and Father of all who is over all and through all and in all" (Ephesians 4:4-6, NASB).

SIX
IT WORKS!
CHARISMATIC
ASSETS

Quite obviously all is not well in the charismatic camp. Of course it never has been and, without being unduly pessimistic, it never will be. But that does not mean that we can do nothing about it.

The critics of the charismatic renewal do not always agree as to the grounds of their criticisms. However, one major line of attack has always been the movement's theology. Many times we have been told, "The charismatic renewal has produced no theology." Professor Walter Hollenweger has often said, as one of their friendliest critics (he was a Pentecostal himself at one time), "What Pentecostals do is of far more significance than what they teach."

What he and other theologians have been saying among themselves is that the effects are magnificent, but the theology is deplorable. It is a bit like the French general's comment after watching the suicide charge of the Light Brigade in the Crimean War: "C'est magnifique, mais ce n'est pas guerre"—"It's great, but it isn't war." Likewise, many an able theologian looking on has said, "It's great, but it doesn't make theological sense."

Therefore, according to these critics, and there are many, charismatics have got to put their theological house in order. Now, I would be the first to agree with the critics that

51

charismatics are not at their best in theological argument, and their dialectic is distinctly hairy at times. There are some weird and wonderful theological explanations which charismatics have advanced to justify themselves. Charismatics are often not their own best friends and can sometimes jump to the defense of their position with the most ungainly and inadequate intellectual weaponry. But that should not cause a retreat on all fronts.

As a matter of fact, I would want to reverse the popularly accepted diagnosis and say that *the charismatic renewal has got its theology about right, but it is its performance which needs most correction.* Whatever may be said about the inadequacy of its theological presentation, its basic theological position is sound. I find it very hard to accept that it is ever possible in any basic sense to produce a magnificent performance (or at least one which is fully Christian) which is based on theological error.

Conversely, it is possible to have sound theology without the complementary performance. But how can one have unsound theology and yet see glorious effects in the lives of people? Of course, it depends a lot on what you mean by theology. But if theology has to do with truth and ultimate reality, that truth is intended to be incarnated in human life and seen in action. If there are no signs or effects in the lives of those who hold to it, one may reasonably doubt the reality of what is being professed, but ought not to reject it out of hand. But if the signs are given and the effects are seen, how can one say "it's not true"?

There may be those who looking at the bulky shape of the Boeing 747 Jumbo Jet on the airport apron, and not knowing any better, would say, "It will never get off the ground." They would be justified in thinking this. But their viewpoint would have to make a very rapid adjustment if they actually saw it lift off the ground and fly off into the distance, and even more so if they were actually to fly in the plane themselves. I think it could be shown without too much difficulty that the actions of charismatics, and the signs which accompany them, are the direct results of the theology they believe. It is, therefore, both unscientific and unfair to applaud charismatic action while at the same time booing their theology.

To the amateur, the Jumbo Jet may look like aerodynamic nonsense. But to the professional it makes aerodynamic sense; otherwise it would never have flown. At first glimpse charismatic teaching, likewise, makes nonsense. But on closer examination, I believe it makes really good sense. Or to put it succinctly: "it works."

Christianity was always meant to work. But what has so often happened in the past has been that Christian faith drifts off either into historical assertions or into prophetic crystal ball gazing, almost entirely neglecting the "here and now," the existential reality of the present moment. Thus, Christians either live in the past or live only for the future. There is little present reality.

Thus, Christians can have their certainties about the past and the historical actions of Jesus Christ, and also about the future and his return in glory. But the bit in between can be obscured with uncertainties. There are also, of course, those who are unsure about most if not all things, and regard it as a serious misdemeanor to claim with certainty anything very seriously—past, present, or future.

The basic theological position of the charismatic renewal, with some variations, is that the God who invaded our world in the person of Jesus Christ nearly 2,000 years ago, and who will come again "in like manner" sometime in the future, still actively moves among his people—and the effects of that real presence are to be expected and experienced in our own lives. They are to be seen and felt in free worship, in signs and wonders, in changed lives and changed circumstances.

In some senses, the charismatic renewal possesses no great incentive to provide a theological justification for its position. The theology which is articulated is surprisingly commonplace. It need not take evangelicals and Catholics by surprise. But there are vital twists to it, which make all the difference.

Charismatic doctrine is "on fire." It takes what others have made dull and tedious and makes it exciting and personal.

This goes some way toward explaining its popularity with the masses. Just as ordinary people flocked to hear Jesus and could listen to him all day and avoided their own "theologians," whom they found out-of-touch with human heartstrings, so charismatic teachers draw together those who are disenchanted with the teachers of our day.

The charismatic renewal has already made a massive contribution to both evangelicalism and Catholicism. For evangelicals it has helped the Word to become "flesh," and for Catholics it has helped to make the sacraments real. Both the Word of God and the sacraments of the Church have a distinct objectivity. The Word of God, unlike heaven and earth, abides forever (Luke 21:33); and the sacraments are administered in the Church in obedience to Jesus Christ until he returns. They do not come and go like so much in our fragile world. But both Word and sacrament need to be made alive to people today. It is the purpose of the Holy Spirit to do that. Because the charismatic renewal has stressed the *experience* of the Holy Spirit, it has followed that the Word has come alive to many, and the sacraments have become exciting encounters with the living God rather than dull and repetitious rituals.

But we need now to look a little more closely at some of the main areas of Christian life and action upon which the charismatic renewal impinges.

CHRISTIAN INITIATION
(See Appendix A, pp. 113-115; Appendix B, pp. 125-128.)

We are plunging into the deep end first. One cannot seriously begin to understand what the charismatic renewal is all about without considering what is called "the baptism in the Holy Spirit." It is here where the point of division is sharpest. Whatever one may say about the baptism in the Holy Spirit, there would be no charismatic renewal today without it. Although much discussion has already taken place over the years, and one is sometimes tempted to turn one's back on the whole business and, if only for the sake of peace and quiet, drop the controversial terminology altogether, I believe this would be a mistake in the light of what God is wanting to say to the Church about it.

Roughly speaking, there are four approaches one can make to the subject.

1. You can take the view that baptism in the Holy Spirit is another way of speaking either of the sacrament of water baptism or the experience of regeneration it pictures. Christian initiation then is completed in baptism, which is the sacramental sign of spiritual regeneration. Every true Christian is, therefore, baptized in the Spirit, and to hold out to Christians a further experience of baptism in the Holy Spirit is confusing and erroneous.

Most of the critics of the theology of charismatic renewal take this particular viewpoint, although this approach is also maintained by some who have clearly articulated sympathies with charismatics and may even be fellow travelers. This viewpoint is taken by Dr. Michael Ramsey in his book *Holy Spirit*: "Here let it only be said that the evidence as interpreted by the weight of New Testament scholarship points to the view that baptism was the sacramental rite given once for all to converts to Jesus as Lord. Subsequent gifts and manifestations of the Spirit in Christian lives are the realization of the meaning and power of the gift which was in baptism once bestowed."

It is also the expressed opinion of John Stott. He writes, "When sinners repent and believe, Jesus not only takes away their sins, but also baptizes them with his Spirit."[12] Or again, "The 'baptism' of the Spirit is identical with the 'gift' of the Spirit. It is one of the *distinctive* blessings of the new covenant, and, because it is an *initial* blessing, it is also a *universal* blessing for members of the covenant. It is part and parcel of belonging to the new age." Another exponent of this view is Simon Tugwell, who writes, "In the New Testament, in the early church, all that Pentecostals understand by 'baptism in the Spirit' is referred quite strictly and simply to what it means to be a Christian at all. The experience of the Spirit is not subsequent to that of conversion and faith; the experience of Pentecost is identical with the baptismal confession that 'Jesus is Lord.' . . . "[13]

The most carefully compiled thesis is that of James G. Dunn in his book *Baptism in the Holy Spirit*.[14] But unlike Dr. Ramsey and Simon Tugwell, Dr. Dunn reduces the significance of water baptism as he expounds the reception of the Spirit (or regeneration as he understands it) as the point of genuine Christian initiation. There are many others who take this position.

2. The second position would be that of the acceptance of the *experience* of "baptism in the Spirit," but the rejection of the terminology and the substitution for it of something else. Thus David C. K. Watson writes, "The term 'baptism' is undoubtedly linked with Christian initiation; and in that sense, at least, every Christian is already baptized in the Spirit."[15] He goes on to suggest another possible use of the phrase, but on the whole comes down heavily for the alternative phrase "to be filled with the Holy Spirit," and then suggests ways by which such an experience can be received.

Cardinal Suenens also takes this view of the experience. He writes, "Our one and only baptism is at the same time both paschal and Pentecostal. To avoid from now on all ambiguity it would be better not to speak of 'baptism in the Spirit' but to look for another expression."[16] (Just to show how difficult it is to get rid of the phrase, the Cardinal himself uses it on the very next page!) Michael Green is another person who follows this line. He accepts the experience of charismatics, but in an article in *Renewal* asks them to "call the rose by some other name; it will smell just as sweet!"[17]

3. The third position is that of the majority of charismatics who both accept the experience *and* the terminology of "baptism in the Spirit." Their viewpoint varies slightly, usually reflecting the particular background or tradition from which they come. This position sympathizes with the older Pentecostal teaching of a two-stage experience and the initial evidence of speaking in tongues as the indubitable sign that the Spirit has

come and filled us. But it departs from it at several important places.

Its teaching is much more of a twin-aspect initiation, rather than a two-stage blessing. It is incorporated into the older structure of sacramental teaching. It sees baptism in the Spirit as part of Christian initiation rather than something completely separate from it. Some would reject altogether the idea that speaking in tongues is the only or necessary evidence of Spirit baptism, though it would accept that it often is. Most of the Roman Catholic charismatics would adopt this position. This is roughly the view of Thomas A. Smail in Chapter 10 of his book *Reflected Glory*,[18] and it is my own position.[19]

4. The fourth position is that of the Pentecostals. Again there is some variety of expression. But the baptism in the Spirit is viewed as something quite distinct from water baptism and regeneration, and most Pentecostals are adamant about speaking in tongues as initial evidence. For them, "it comes with the package." There are also some neo-Pentecostals who adopt this position. Perhaps the best known is Dennis Bennett.[20]

Rather than do a detailed examination of what can be said about each of these positions, I am going to share how I see the question of terminology, and why I have consistently stuck to the phrase "baptism in the Spirit" even though aware of the emotive nature of it. The name is important, and I believe we need to face up to the theological difficulties and not shirk them.

The phrase "to be baptized in the Spirit" is probably used exclusively in the New Testament to describe the event of Pentecost. There are only seven texts in the New Testament in which the phrase occurs. Four of these are in the Gospels and, with slight variation, are part of John the Baptist's comments during his ministry (Matthew 3:11; Mark 1:8; Luke 3:16; John 1:33). Two references are in Acts (1:5; 11:16). In Paul's letters there is but one reference (1 Corinthians 12:13). The four Gospel references refer to the ministry of Christ, fulfilled (according to Acts 1:5 and by inference Acts 11:16) on the Day of Pentecost. The other reference (1 Corinthians 12:13) is the only one which is not directly related to the Day of Pentecost.

First Corinthians 12:13 is one of those texts which, though simple enough to interpret within its own context, has almost collapsed under the weight put upon it in the context of charismatic controversies. Not a few have sought to deduce from this text that all Christians are baptized in the Spirit. Does not Paul say, "for by [or in] one Spirit we were *all* baptized into one body, whether Jews or Greeks, whether slaves or free, and *we* were *all* made to drink of one Spirit" (NASB)? Whatever interpretation we give to this text, what does seem certain is that Paul does not seem to have used the phrase "baptism in the Spirit" in the sense in which it is used today by charismatics.

The argument from silence is never conclusive. But in view of the charismatic nature of Paul's ministry and the many references in his writings to the Holy Spirit, it is of some significance that he only once uses the phrase, and does so in 1 Corinthians in a very different way to that employed by Pentecostals and charismatics today.

My own deduction from the evidence we have in the New Testament is that the early Christians set a pattern, which was followed reasonably consistently until deep in the nineteenth century (with the advent of the holiness movements), of using the phrase "baptism in the Holy Spirit" only to describe the Pentecost event. We could conjecture that the reason for so doing was in order not to confuse it with water baptism. This is not necessarily to say that it is wrong for us to use it. It is only saying that the phrase, which does in my opinion describe the *anointing* rather than the *birth* of the Church, was not used in this contemporary sense during much of the Church's history.

The reality of Pentecostal experience has been part of the life of the Church. But for various reasons, which we can only guess, it was seldom, if ever, called by this name. (As an aside, it is ironical that some use it today as another way of describing water baptism. In so doing, they confuse two realities which were distinct in the New Testament, though closely—not inseparably—related; namely, water baptism and the receiving of the power or anointing of the Spirit.)

It would seem also that some today see water baptism as completed initiation, whereas the New Testament sees baptism as a constellation of realities and events which in totality marked Christian initiation, and of which water baptism was but one part. Early Christian leaders and teachers would have been anxious to discourage the idea of several stages or initiations because of the influence of Gnostics and others who stressed a whole chain of initiations into higher and higher spiritual life. But then again, Pentecost was to them a part of the one Christian initiation, *not the whole of it,* and baptism in the Spirit would not in their thinking and practice have been equated with either conversion or regeneration.

The nonuse of the expression "baptism in the Spirit" in the New Testament Church should not preclude our using it today, since it is scriptural terminology and describes the empowering of the Spirit with a vividness which is in great contrast to the drabness surrounding the theory and practice of so much Christian initiation today. There are, in addition, special reasons why we may use the expression today, provided we make it clear that it is neither a new sacrament, nor a "second blessing" distinct from Christian initiation. There is less danger today of the Gnostic approach. On the contrary, the chief danger lies in the opposite direction, a cut-and-dried approach to initiation which says, "I've got it all and have need of nothing."

Dr. Martyn Lloyd-Jones, for many years the minister of famous Westminster Chapel in London, once asked in a sermon, " 'Got it all?' Well, if you have 'got it all' I simply ask in the name of God, why are you as you are? If you have got it all, why are you so unlike the New Testament Christians? Got it all! Got it at your conversion! Well, where is it, I ask?"[21] It may be for this very reason, to shock complacent Christians, that some of us have been led to take this phrase out of mothballs at such a time as this.

Nor is there too much danger, as in the first century, of Spirit baptism being confused with water baptism. The whole subject of water baptism is confused today, but not as it was in the early church. There is sometimes a deadly sacramentalism which puts too much weight on the rite of water baptism, in practice ignoring the action of the Holy Spirit, which from earliest Christian times was regarded as crucial to the total baptism experience.

In all this the popular use of the phrase "baptism in the Spirit" today has been instrumental in bringing many evangelicals out of their cozy and lackadaisical view of initiation, and sacramentalists from their quasi-magical approach to water baptism. We should be thankful for this and not be too hasty in throwing out the expression before it has completed its work.

For some, the expression "filled with the Holy Spirit" is preferred to that of "baptism in the Holy Spirit." In Acts 2:4 it is used to describe what happened to the Church on the Day of Pentecost. It is, therefore, perfectly legitimate to use it as an alternative to "baptism in the Holy Spirit."

But there are some snags. This expression is used in the New Testament to describe a whole variety of actions of the Holy Spirit, and, indeed, mostly of a noninitiatory nature. In Ephesians 5:18 Paul urges his readers to be (literally) "continuously filled with the Holy Spirit." But it would be unthinkable to urge Christians to be continuously baptized in the Spirit. That would be equivalent to drowning!

Besides, being "filled with the Spirit" has strong ethical overtones to it, which creates problems in its use. It is much harder to say "I am a Spirit-filled believer" than to say "I am Spirit-baptized." Spirit baptism does not partake of degrees, whereas the notion of being Spirit-filled does. Another objection is that "Spirit-filled" is a much more subjective concept than "Spirit-baptized." "Filling" describes an inward experience, whereas "baptism" describes an outward one. For these reasons I prefer the terminology of Spirit baptism.

In the final analysis we will have to live with the expression "baptism in the Spirit." We have to face the facts; namely, that it would be quite impossible, even if it were desirable, to dismiss the term "baptism in the Spirit" or attempt to prevent its use. It is better to use the term properly and to safeguard it from the several misunderstandings which have surrounded it. It has now become part of the settled vocabulary of renewal, and whatever anyone else may say about it, it will go on being used. The best way forward is to explain it more clearly and thus save it from misuse and misunderstanding, while at the same time letting it continue its effective ministry of disturbing comfortable evangelical pews and pulpits and rocking placid sacramental boats.

Kilian McDonnell in the book *The Holy Spirit and Power*[22] sees the focus of the charismatic renewal in the phrase "baptism in the Spirit." He argues for the retention of the "baptism in the Spirit" terminology, but distinguishes between the theological use of the expression (which he rejects on the grounds that all Christians are baptized in the Spirit) and the experiential, which is the way some are using it in the charismatic renewal. This Roman Catholic scholar is prepared to accept the terminology, while at the same time explaining what it means.

The effect of charismatic theology is to fill out the whole doctrine of salvation. Baptism in the Spirit (in the charismatic sense) does not add to our salvation, and the absence of it in our experience does not mean we are not "saved." But it amplifies and makes the effects of our salvation far more substantial. The dynamic of this can be seen in the many ramifications of charismatic renewal. Charismatics have, for example, pioneered new areas of so-called "inner healing," and the ministry of women has been particularly effective here. The pioneers include Agnes Sanford, Anne White, and Ruth Carter Stapleton, the sister of President Carter, to name only three.

Then there has been the increasing use of exorcism as a means of deliverance which charismatics have pioneered. Here men seem to excel, and one could mention the names of Derek Prince, Don Basham, and Maxwell Whyte, who have been the front-runners in this area. We could also mention the proliferation of Christian communities, such as the Church of the Redeemer, Houston and its child the Communities of Celebration, and the famous Roman Catholic Community of the Word of God in Ann Arbor, Michigan.

The dynamic source of spiritual power in individuals has not been allowed to remain encapsulated in charismatics, to become not much more than a super ego trip. On the contrary, it has issued forth like a river swollen with floodwaters, and has become a potent source of inspiration for a great deal of creative ministry in the Church and to the world.

WORSHIP
(See Appendix A, pp. 117, 118; Appendix B, page 129.)

Evangelical worship tends to be word-centered. In its more extreme forms, evangelicalism treats worship as a kind of "filler" for the main purpose for which Christians meet, which is to listen to sermons. Worship takes a very secondary role to that of the reading and exposition of the Scriptures.

We can see something of this in evangelical hymns of the last hundred years. They tend to be either doctrinal expositions in verse, or pious and self-centered and individualized acts of devotion. There have been a few prophetic voices in recent years decrying this devaluation of such a precious activity, particularly the voice and pen of A. W. Tozer.

At the same time, evangelism has passed through a phase in which worship has been downgraded and evangelism regarded as mainly a mental exercise in which one delivers a well thought out lecture with a view to a thoughtful commitment to Jesus Christ. Anything else has been regarded as "emotionalism," or taking unfair advantage of people by stirring them up so that they make emotional rather than intellectual decisions to follow Jesus Christ.

The enormous power of worship to make God real to people has been almost totally neglected. One well-known English evangelist, David Watson, in his excellent book *I Believe in Evangelism*, would differ from this kind of thinking and sees worship as an integral part of effective evangelism. "When Christians are to be found really worshiping God, loving him, serving him, excited with him, and when their worship makes them into a caring community of love, then questions will certainly be asked, leading to excellent opportunities for sharing the good news of Christ."[23]

The charismatic renewal has done much to restore worship to its central place in the Church. But there are features which are comparatively new and different from, say, hearty Methodist singing. Worshipers, for instance, are more active and *physical* in their worship—tapping their feet, clapping their hands, raising their arms, and even dancing in the aisles.

The music too is different. If you glance through *Sound of Living Waters* and *Fresh Sounds*,[24] you will see a great variety of songs which are the expression in verse and song of spiritual renewal in people's hearts. Almost all are God-centered, and corporate rather than individual expressions of worship. Their words are simple. There is a marked absence of Victorian sentimentality. Sankey finds no place in these modern songbooks. The music is melodious and of comparatively good quality. The songs are eminently singable. Anyone who has been to the average charismatic prayer meeting will find it easy to contrast it with anything else. Whether one would say it is better is a matter of opinion, but that it is different and new is beyond contradiction.

Roman Catholics have had one important advantage over evangelicals; namely, the influence of the liturgical movement, which has barely touched evangelicals. This movement, together with others (such as the Focolare movement, marriage encounter, and particularly the Cursillo movement), influenced Roman Catholics before the charismatic movement arrived on the scene. One effect has been the desire to express worship freely and relevantly and to blow away traditions which have, like cobwebs, been obscuring the light. The influence of these movements can be clearly seen in the worship of Roman Catholic charismatics.

So one can say that Roman Catholics did have at least a head start on their evangelical friends. But Roman Catholicism is much more worship orientated than evangelicalism anyway, and it tends to be more "physical" as well. But the inhibiting factor in Roman Catholicism has been the individualism encouraged by the tendency of many Catholics to view attendance at Mass as being the fulfillment of their Christian duty, a ceremony many of them attend with monotonous regularity, making what is really a private communion, almost totally unrelated to the rest of the Body of Christ present. Sacramentalism has taken the place of a real commitment, in the totality of life (of which Mass is one expression), to both Christ and his people.

But what Roman Catholics in the renewal have come to see is that Mass does not take you any higher than you are "on average" during the week. If you are almost a total failure as a Christian person Monday to Saturday, Sunday Mass is not going to make you a success. It is in seeing this that many Catholics have found release in worship and praise through their charismatic experience.

And it has led them, as it always does, to an enhanced appreciation and respect for the sacraments. The sacraments become what they were always meant to be to us: some of God's chief means of grace to pilgrim Christians. If for evangelicals the Bible becomes a new book, for Roman Catholics the sacraments become altogether more wonderful than they ever were before.

EVANGELISM

Church history, evangelical and Roman Catholic, is full of glorious sagas of missionary endeavors. Evangelism, albeit with different emphases, has been a major factor in the traditions of both. But while it is possible to see a Roman Catholicism almost bereft of individual evangelistic concern, personal evangelism has always been part of the very lifeblood of evangelicals. It would be as impossible to imagine an evangelical who does not at least have some concern for preaching the gospel and converting unbelievers, as it would a Roman

Catholic who has little or no concern for the sacraments. What then has charismatic experience done to both?

For the evangelical, at least as far as I have observed, his attitude to the world often changes. From being judgmental, the evangelical acquires a more Christlike compassion for those trapped in the web of the world, the flesh, and the devil. This was what dramatically and suddenly happened to me when I was baptized in the Spirit in 1962. I was at the time chaplain to five of London's large department stores. My work took me frequently into these stores. My "parish" was totally dedicated to mammon.

That is not to say that it was necessarily corrupt or that those involved in it were not providing a service to the public. Many of the people I met were decent, honest, and hard-working. But they were there to make money—not that there is anything wrong about that, but for some the whole atmosphere and business of buying and selling had made them basically materialistic.

Brought up in the evangelical fold to be distinctly critical of all "worldliness," my attitude to the people I met in the stores was colored. But when I was baptized in the Spirit this changed. I found I had a love for people which was quite different from what it had been. I found myself thinking the best of them, rather than assuming the worst. I was no longer their judge, only their friend. This was indeed the Spirit of Jesus Christ, who was called by his enemies and detractors "the friend of sinners," controlling my thoughts and attitudes.

Wherever I have gone in the charismatic renewal, I have found the same thing happening to countless other people. One of the reasons why the movement has spread so fast and so far is that it has been prepared to accept people without demur who smoke cigarettes at prayer meetings and drink alcohol at conferences. In actual fact what charismatics have learned to do, without perhaps realizing it, is to preach the gospel without its cultural baggage of social and moral taboos. In this respect it has been highly successful.

Roman Catholics are not entirely free from those taboos. But on the whole, perhaps because from the evangelical standpoint they have been less puritanical in their approach to such matters as cigarette smoking, drinking, the use of cosmetics, going to the theatre, etc., many Roman Catholics have not had the same hang-ups. Of course, it could be said plainly that they are more worldly than evangelicals. If that is true, then it needs to be analyzed a little more closely. Roman Catholics are brought up on natural as well as redemption theology, whereas many evangelicals are not. Putting it more simply, Roman Catholics tend to begin with the doctrine of creation and the goodness of man as originally created, and only then begin to talk about redemption. Evangelicals, on the other hand, begin with sin and take a person right on from there to redemption through the Cross.

In fact, evangelical theology is inclined both to leave Christ hanging on the Cross or cold in the tomb and people condemned in their sin. Thus, Roman Catholics naturally have a more hopeful attitude in regard to their fellow human beings and are inclined to make beneficial assumptions about their eternal well-being, while the evangelical seeks to bring them under conviction of sin. Granted, not all see it this way and there would appear to be grounds for either side.

But what Roman Catholics have found through their involvement in charismatic renewal is different: they have discovered the art of personal evangelism. They have become "soul winners," to use an evangelical cliché. Ralph Martin, for example, in his book *Unless the Lord Builds the House*, [25] is saying in so many words that many Roman Catholics need to be evangelized. He sees the university campuses of the United States as mission fields, much as Campus Crusade for Christ or Inter-Varsity do. Ralph Martin is a prominent leader of the charismatic renewal in the United States. He and others like Steve Clark, in setting up the now famous Life in the Spirit seminars, have made it clear that they regard an evangelical conversion or commitment to be essential to Christian living or life in the Spirit.

Thus in the Team Manual (edited by Steve Clark) for the Life in the Spirit seminars, there is a seminar on "Salvation."[26] The goal is described as: "to help people see the momentousness of Christianity, to help them to understand the basic Christian message (what Jesus has done and will do for them), to help them to realize the need for a serious decision." The basis of the seminar itself is the realization of sin, and God's remedy in Jesus. It is all good, sound evangelical doctrine.

In some ways one could say that Roman Catholics have rediscovered the gospel through charismatic renewal, while evangelicals have found a new way of reaching people—in love rather than judgment. But what it means for both is that joint evangelism is a possibility in a way that it was not before. One is finding increasingly that Roman Catholic students are participating in Christian fellowships at universities, and so working with evangelical students in personal and corporate evangelism. In New Zealand it has not been unknown for Inter-Varsity college leaders to be Roman Catholics. At the same time evangelicals are finding themselves invited to priest retreats and Catholic parishes to talk and instruct Catholics in personal evangelism.

But there is something else which both evangelical and Catholic charismatics have rediscovered—the itinerant ministry. Both evangelicalism and Roman Catholicism have honorable traditions in this regard. The Pilgrim fathers, the Methodist lay preachers, the Franciscans, the Lollards are examples from both traditions of men who were moved by the Holy Spirit to travel, in some cases great distances, to fulfil their ministries or, in the case of the Pilgrim fathers, to have the freedom to worship and live in the ways their consciences would allow.

The charismatic renewal happened to coincide with the jet revolution, which has meant cheap long-distance travel for all. Charismatics have jetted around the world to share their good news with anyone willing to listen. Both Roman Catholic and evangelical charismatics by the hundreds have toured the earth and shared together in a stupendous outreach which has brought renewal to almost every corner of the globe.

ECUMENISM
(See Appendix B, page 123.)

We have been witnesses of one of the greatest miracles of the twentieth century. There have previously been some encouragements in terms of Christian unity related to church union schemes, and many disappointments also. But quite suddenly the greatest chasm of all seemed to be bridged for the first time. The charismatic renewal has brought together Christians of every variety.

In 1977 the Kansas City Conference gathered together for the first time in history the various streams of the Christian Church in general and of the charismatic renewal in particular. Admittedly, they mostly came from the Roman Catholic Church and the independent churches. According to the statistics, 49 percent were Roman Catholic and 30 percent from independent charismatic churches. But there were also present members of the mainstream Protestant denominations: Episcopal, Methodist, Lutheran, Presbyterian, Baptist, some of the Pentecostal churches, groups of so-called Messianic Jews, etc. Nothing has ever been seen like it before.

But the significance of the conference is to be found not only in who came, but also in how it was organized. All the denominational fellowships shared in the planning beforehand on an equal footing. So Roman Catholics sat down with people who belonged to no denomination, Episcopalians shared with Mennonites, and Baptists with Messianic Jews. There have been great ecumenical conferences before, particularly those organized by the World Council of Churches. But never before has such a cross section of people and causes been joined together in this way.

One of the pioneers of this new ecumenism has been David du Plessis. He calls it "economical ecumenism." David crashed through the ecumenical barrier when he visited the New York offices of the World Council of Churches in 1952. For the first time a high-ranking Pentecostal had made contact with the WCC. David was pioneering a new ecumenism which does not wait to be invited, but shares in order to witness to the things one believes.

David du Plessis has since 1952 been used more than anyone else to bring Christians together in charismatic renewal. His advances were made not only to the WCC, but in time to the Vatican itself. He was to be the only Pentecostal observer at the second Ecumenical Council in Rome, and over the years has been involved with many Roman Catholics in the renewal.

The new ecumenism essentially trusts in the Holy Spirit to guide and to lead into all truth. It believes that Christian love initiates, and that we need to have our prejudices and fears removed so that we can take that initiative. Charismatics may be inclined to gloss over some of the differences and to be reluctant to engage in the discipline and hardship of mutual dialogue. They may assume rather too much. But they are normally motivated by a great love for their fellow Christians and a passionate belief that in Jesus Christ we are already one. They want to demonstrate that essential unity not only in the conference setting, which is easy, but in life and ministry.

So we have seen the increasing development of ecumenical communities and ecumenical sharing and experimentation at the local level. At a time when the ecumenical movement itself has been rather dragging its feet, the charismatic renewal has brought new hope and expectations to many.

COMMUNITY
(See Appendix A, page 119, 120; Appendix B, page 130-132.)

There has been an almost universal defectiveness in Christendom in the experience of Christian community. Evangelicalism has come from the seedbed of individualism, which was a conspicuous product of the society which came into being at the Reformation and of the social upheavals which came in the period before and after the Reformation. The private conscience of the individual was deemed of greater importance than the group. The right of private and personal judgment was strongly asserted.

In the Western world, we have seen in more recent years the lifting up of the nuclear family (at the expense often of the larger family of the Church and the world) and the decline of the extended family as a basis for normal living. People have been encouraged to live in lonely isolation, and other social and economic pressures have had their effect on the family, reducing it in size and increasing the gap between it and the rest of society.

Although Roman Catholicism has seen the expression of corporate Christianity in the spread and development of the religious orders, nevertheless even this aspect of Catholic spirituality has in some ways proved to be counterproductive. The tendency has been for Catholics to put all their eggs into the one basket, and for those who have not joined a religious order to regard themselves as "let off the hook," so to speak. Thus the local parish has tended to be a kind of mass station, rather than a family of God's people.

But the charismatic renewal has begun to change some of these attitudes. There has been a growing awareness among both evangelicals and Roman Catholics of this basic weakness. The charismatic renewal has not been alone in influencing the whole Church to move in another direction. The Focalare movement is a good example of a vision, given long before the charismatic renewal started, which has influenced many Catholics to think corporately without necessarily joining a religious order.

Evangelicals, sometimes through the influence of the charismatic renewal and sometimes through other agencies, have become aware of their lack in this area. Thus, at the National Evangelical Anglican Congress at Nottingham in 1977 the Statement on "Church as Community" reads: "We recognize that a necessary stress on the need for individual response to Jesus Christ has sometimes obscured a recognition of the corporate nature of our commitment to Christ, to which the New Testament gives clear witness. We believe that the church is an organic structure within which we depend on each other for Christian life, growth and service."[27]

In the charismatic renewal in the Roman Catholic Church, one of the major thrusts has been the building up of a whole network of communities—sometimes people living together, sometimes people having a commitment to each other which is short of this. Many of them are called "covenant communities," in that the members covenant with one another in a simple but radical way. It was the Church of the Redeemer, Houston that pioneered this new style of Christian living. Although an Episcopal church, the Roman Catholics accepted its basic principles and adapted them to their own needs.

The evangelical world has not gone this far, although there are signs of this beginning to happen. The Sojourners in Washington, D.C., are an interesting example of a group coming from an evangelical position, taking a radical social stance, and at the same time developing a community life-style. They and other similar groups may well be pioneers whom other evangelicals will follow. Through much of the evangelical stream of Christian life, there is a ground swell which is influencing many in the direction of a much more corporate orientation.

Evangelicals are beginning to take the Church seriously, without losing their concern for individual conversions. It would be a sad mistake to imagine that the two are mutually exclusive. A right understanding of the Church in its corporate dimension, and the development of true brotherly love, gives to those outside the Church family a greater incentive to join in, and to those inside the Church family a greater desire to draw them in.

MINISTRY
(See Appendix B, page 132-138.)

One of the most conspicuous marks of the Holy Spirit's work in charismatic renewal has been its insistence on what we have come to call "every-member ministry." The charismatic renewal is by no means unique in its stress on this, although it is probably true to say that there is more scope for, and resulting evidence of this New Testament principle in, the charismatic renewal than anywhere else in the Church. Charismatics do not pay lip service to this principle.

Not a few have been drawing our attention to the multitudinous gifts of the Spirit that the New Testament tells us about. But where are they to be seen in action in the contemporary Church? Where are the prophets, and how often are services and meetings punctuated with relevant and heart-searching prophecies? Are the sick being healed? Are people being liberated from unseen malevolent spiritual forces? Are gifts of leadership developing within our churches, or is power in the hands of a few? Do we still find that most of the work is being done in reality by a dedicated few, while the majority sit and listen? How far are evangelistic gifts present in the Church, and how effective are they in reaching the outside world? At least one can see the beginnings of the every-member ministry in churches where there is charismatic renewal.

Both the evangelical and Catholic worlds have in different ways been inhibited from really developing this principle to its fullest extent. Evangelicals have tended to see ministry almost exclusively in terms of preaching and teaching. This naturally limits the scope of ministry to a few people, and is inevitably lopsided in its influence on the local church. With the increasing demand for an "intellectual" ministry, and with many judging the effectiveness of a church almost exclusively by the minister's performance in the pulpit, the every-member ministry is restricted.[28]

But there are healthy signs of change in the evangelical world. Three times in the Nottingham Statement,[29] Anglican evangelicals in Britain affirmed their commitment to the implications of this principle. In the section on "Church as Community" there is a stated "commitment to every-member ministry (including oversight). . . . " Under "Christian maturing" there is the statement, "We believe that Christian ministry, which is the privilege of every member of the Body of Christ, is intended to bring the whole Christian community into maturity." In the section "Ministry and Mission" we read: "Clerical professionalism has gravely inhibited the proper development of the diversity of ministries. We deplore the prevalent pattern of 'one-man ministries,' which are good neither for the man nor for the parish. . . . "

Everywhere in the evangelical world there is a questioning of old presuppositions, and a new openness to ministries which have not been in evidence before. Just as evangelicals today see their ministry to the world in terms of social action as well as evangelistic outreach, so they are more and more seeing their ministry in the Church in wider terms than the teaching and preaching ministry of the old style where there is no comeback or dialogue.

Prophetic and counseling ministries are in one sense a "ministry of the Word," but are different from a straightforward exposition of Scripture to a largely passive audience. Evangelicals have tended to be good speakers but poor listeners. This imbalance is being corrected, and the charismatic renewal is playing a part in this.

If an overemphasis on preaching has been the strongest factor inhibiting evangelicals from the every-member ministry principle, in the Roman Catholic world it has been a false kind of "priestliness." Clericalism has not affected Roman Catholicism quite in the same way that it has evangelicalism. The demonstration of this can be seen in the way in which the Catholic charismatic renewal has developed.

Whereas the movement within the Anglican and Protestant Churches has tended to develop with clerical or ministerial leadership, the Roman Catholics have (at least in the United States) had predominantly lay leadership. Bishops and priests have tended to bring up the rear rather than take the lead and initiative. Clericalism is on the whole stronger in the Protestant world than it is in the Roman Catholic. It is true that there are certain spheres of ministry which are exclusively "priestly." But these are very limited, and the twentieth century has seen a number of powerful lay movements in the Roman Catholic Church where, even if some of the pioneering has been done by priests or members of religious orders, most of the inspiration in extending it has come from lay leaders. Examples include the Legion of Mary, the Focalare movement, the Cursillo movement, marriage encounter, and the charismatic renewal.

One factor in this may be the rule of celibacy for Roman Catholic priests and religious leaders. This means that whereas many of those who feel called to marriage in the Protestant world are also ordained, there tend to be many Roman Catholics who, although they possess gifts of leadership and feel called to marriage and family life, are not able to be ordained because of the rules of their Church. But it is still true that clericalism is an inhibiting factor in the Roman Catholic Church, and where priestly domination still pertains the lay person has little or no option but to set up his own prayer group or community to further the work of renewal in his neighborhood.

This means that although the charismatic renewal has furthered or introduced the every-member principle to some parts of the Roman Catholic world, the ministry tends to polarize into the "clerical" or "priestly" ministry, which is sacramental and is not open to lay people, and the "charismatic," which is free and spontaneous and open to all. This raises all kinds of questions, the answers to which lie outside the scope of this book.

We have looked at some of the ways in which God seems to have used the charismatic movement for the benefit of the whole Church. The movement itself is very much on the move. Being a moving target it is difficult to "hit." What may be true of it one moment could be false to it the next. We now need to balance the assets of the movement with its liabilities. We do so aware of the fact that the "balance sheet" is difficult to arrive at, for just as there are no fixed assets, so there are no fixed liabilities.

A good example of this is the most famous controversy so far—the so-called "discipleship" affair of 1975-76. Here what seemed like a heavy liability was turned very quickly into at least a partial asset. But that story belongs to the next part of the book.

SEVEN
HOT-DOG
CHRISTIANITY?
CHARISMATIC
LIABILITIES

In the last section I expressed my conviction that the charismatic renewal is not only making an important contribution in what it is *doing*, but also in what it is *saying* about the contemporary church situation. Its theology, even if inadequately formulated, is about correct. But its greater weakness lies in what it sometimes builds on this theology. If the charismatic renewal and its close relatives in the Pentecostal movement are to draw closer to the evangelical and Roman Catholic worlds, then they need to come to terms with their weaknesses and find ways of overcoming them.

Results do not prove anything. Success does not justify the methods which may have been used to bring it about. It seems too that it is often not the charismatic renewal in principle which evangelicals and Roman Catholics object to, but the excesses and aberrations which are sometimes associated with it. This is where change is required.

There is not much need to tinker around with the theology of the renewal. No doubt there is room for improvement. But the differences between charismatic and other Christian theologies should be able to be contained within the frontiers of a pluralistic unity which is inevitable if we are taking Christian unity seriously and are realistic about it.

If there is one main point of controversy in the charismatic renewal, it lies in the area of *authority*. Most of the major differences stem from this, and most of the aberrations come from this area. There is the question of so-called "deliverance" ministry, and the authority which one exercises over evil spirits. There is the so-called discipleship issue which split the charismatic renewal in 1975, though most of the breach has since been made good. There has been the controversy over water baptism, which in a sense concerns authority, the authority to baptize and, as some would call it, to rebaptize.

There have also been the usual problems associated with personalities, of which the charismatic renewal certainly has no monopoly. There have also been many questions about the place of the miraculous in ministry. "Miracle services," such as those conducted by the late Kathryn Kuhlman, raise many questions. But again the main point of issue seems to be authority. Can we demand of God that he do what we believe he ought to do? Is he in authority or are we?

HOT-DOG CHRISTIANITY

"Hot-dog" is a name which has been given to a certain brand of tennis. The growth of tennis professionalism has led to some "playing to the gallery." Illie Nastase is perhaps the greatest example of this kind of tennis. The crowd loves it and will pay big money to see it. It is not necessarily skillful, but it entertains people. Gimmicky strokes may not even win the point. But they bring laughter and enjoyment, which for some is at least as important as the tennis itself.

The charismatic renewal has produced its own brands of "hot-dog" Christianity. Sometimes there is expert showmanship. Large crowds gather. Spectacular things happen. Everyone is thrilled. The crowds disperse talking about the miracles they have seen. But what it all adds up to in the final analysis is another matter altogether. The miracle service has become a central point in some streams of the charismatic renewal. The most illustrious example of this was the late Kathryn Kuhlman.

78

I was present at several of Miss Kuhlman's meetings. I was able to go to one of the great Sunday afternoon rallies at the Shrine Auditorium in Los Angeles. I was also present at Melodyland in Anaheim when she had one of her miracle services. I also met her personally. She was so much part of the charismatic renewal and had such a large following that it is worth pondering what it was that drew the crowds and what was the secret of the flow of miracles that came from her meetings.

I cannot claim to have known her very well. Even those who knew her intimately would say that in some ways she remained an enigma to the end of her life. The revelations of her past which are revealed in Jamie Buckingham's biography of her, *Daughter of Destiny*,[30] may have dented her image a bit. If this is an accurate record of this remarkable woman's life (according to Jamie Buckingham, he was told by Kathryn before her death, "Tell it all, Jamie"), then it may be possible to put one's finger on a key to her life. The private life of Kathryn, her extravagances, her meanness toward her staff, her periodic ego trips, and her unwillingness to face or even accept the hard facts of the failure of her marriage reveal much human weakness and sin. Yet God chose to use her in strange and decisive ways.

It may well be possible to understand why she behaved as she did. Her upbringing with a father she adored and a mother who flogged her would account for some of that. The key to her success was her faith in a God of mercy and her ability to identify with sin-sick people. She could get to the gut level quicker than most. Her gospel was theologically limited, her teaching abysmally inadequate. But she loved people and she loved God. She usually faltered when she tried to explain how she ticked spiritually. She saw abundant success when she pursued her simple straightforward course. She was someone through whom the little person could see and find God, even if some almost made her their god. She with all her faults and defects was used by God—and we can be too.

She always seemed to me to have a disdain of officialdom. At times she almost dared her critics to try to stop the flow of charismatic power. She gave of herself unstintingly. When she died she could have no successor. She was unique. There are those who claim to have received the Kuhlman mantle of power, but there will never be another Kathryn Kuhlman. She got away with it, whereas many others never did and never will. There was always something that just saved her from becoming a charlatan.

But the problem of "hot-dog" Christianity remains. It is one of the more serious drawbacks to the charismatic renewal. There are minds which are bent in such a way that they can only really think in terms of the miracle. I remember once in the United States attending a service in which a layman prayed that the Lord would multiply the world's oil resources much as Jesus multiplied the loaves and fishes. There are always those who see miracles as a convenient way of ignoring what the Lord might be saying about something else. There is often a narrow line between true faith which believes in miracles and human selfishness which demands them.

The charismatic renewal has produced a rash of miracle workers who tout their wares like traveling salesmen. There are the word of knowledge performers, slayers in the Spirit, leg lengtheners, and charismatic dentists, to name just a few. My own observations convince me that miracles have been genuinely performed, but that all too many use harmful techniques which make God into our servant, rather than us into his. The Lord, according to some, is there at our beck and call. He is obedient to our demands, rather than we to his. Often there is no real link between the miracle performed and the reason God has worked.

Perhaps we could look more closely at one of these ministries, the lengthening of legs. I have no doubts in my own mind that sometimes God has done this. My wife Jeanne has, for example, experienced it. I am equally convinced that others have taken this to an unreasonable extreme. One has heard it said that *everyone* has one leg longer than the other. This is medically true, just as it is true that we have one arm longer than the other and that one side of our face is different from the other. It is also true that *sometimes* the effect of this so far as our unequal legs are concerned is that we have back troubles and other physical problems. But the difference between the length of the average person's legs is so small that it can barely be measured.

How is it then that so many claim that they have actually seen a leg grow to the same length as the other? I am not questioning cases where either for congenital reasons or as a result of an accident, one leg is *obviously* shorter than the other. I have been present when a woman who had one leg shorter than the other following a hip operation was prayed for. The hospital had actually given her a shoe which was built up in order to compensate for this. But after prayer the leg grew and there was a noticeable difference.

"Hot-dog" Christianity exists when, for the sake of entertainment and thrills, claims are made which cannot be substantiated and are based on spurious foundations. The sight of scores of people all being prayed for so that their legs might grow, when the difference is microscopically small, and then claiming they have *seen* the difference between their legs, and their legs growing to compensate, is unfortunate, and a hindrance to the drawing together of God's people in harmony and love.

The practice of "slaying with the Spirit" was in my opinion the least attractive aspect of the public ministry of Kathryn Kuhlman and an unfortunate legacy of hers to the charismatic renewal, for many are imitating her. It has become a standard technique with some. As with leg lengthening, there are no doubt genuine cases of people who fall on the floor under the influence of the Holy Spirit. But equally, there are false experiences. The term "slaying with the Spirit," which came originally from early Pentecostalism, is an unfortunate description. Nowhere in the New Testament are we told that the Holy Spirit "slays" anyone. Like Jesus Christ, he "gives life" (2 Corinthians 3:6, NASB).

It is true there are examples in the New Testament of people falling down before the Lord. Saul of Tarsus did it outside Damascus. But his was a response of awe and wonder coupled with conviction of sin. John did the same on the island of Patmos, according to his description in Revelation 1:17, when he saw the Lord. But the contemporary experience is usually neither a response of conviction of sin or of "seeing the Lord."

Like lengthening of legs, the experience of "slaying with the Spirit" has been exploited by some and developed into a technique. For some, the sensation of seeing bodies strewn all over the platform is worth traveling hundred of miles. It helps to draw the crowds. Frankly, it needs "demythologizing." Myth must be distinguished from the reality, which is certainly sometimes there.

It needs retitling too. Francis MacNutt has found that there are times when people are being healed and find themselves falling to the ground. He prefers to call it "resting in the Spirit." I have also known occasions when people have come suddenly under conviction and have found their legs weakening, and down they go. As something spontaneous, taking everyone by surprise, it has an authentic ring about it. But to have prearranged workers stationed behind people to catch them as they fall is not very convincing.

STAR TREKS

The "star system" is a well-established part of American life. It is not only required in "show biz"; it is an essential aspect of other areas of life. In the secular sphere, a new name for it is "charisma." It is that indefinable "something" which sets a person apart from lesser mortals. It may involve what we call "sex appeal," but that is not the kernel of the matter. In practical terms, it can catch votes in political elections, sometimes more than any other single factor. Life is so governed by it today (and the mass media have contributed a great deal to its influence) that although a person with so-called "charisma" might not necessarily win an election, it is now unlikely that any person without it would win a major election in a Western country.

It is probably true that "charisma" in the secular sense can be taught and can be successfully imitated. One could almost think of setting up schools to train people to be "charismatic." But even with the best training available a large number of people, by reason of their defective personalities or lack of motivation, would never be "charismatic." That's not bad news either. Who wants to be anyway? The ones who want it often produce it. It may win you friends, but it will certainly make you enemies. You may well achieve success, but there will certainly be accompanying sorrows as well.

But we are not here primarily concerned with the *secular* "charismatic movement." Our problem comes where there is a mixture of the sacred and secular. There is no doubt that the "star system" which is universally accepted in most of the world is also a key factor in the Christian Church, and in the charismatic renewal. This renewal movement stresses, among other things, the rediscovery of spiritual or charismatic gifts. And because it emphasizes the "every-member" ministry principle, every Christian is potentially, in that sense, "charismatic."

But here there is a complicating factor. The secular "star system" also sometimes operates among Christians. As a result, the charismatic renewal has bred a new generation of stargazers. As the "stars" trek around the earth, their followers gather in large numbers to see "the great thing that has come to pass." This means that "charisma" is not, for many, simply an anointing or gift from God for ministry and service. It is also the projection of a personality, with much of the glamor and publicity which goes with it. Thus, Kathryn Kuhlman played a public role like that of a Hollywood film star, and lived in private a similar kind of life (although certainly never guilty of the kind of immorality often associated with show-biz personalities).

It is not my purpose at this stage to condemn the "star system" outright, as applied to Christian leaders. To some extent there will always be something of the world's attitudes and outlook reflected in the Christian world also. But my plea would be for a careful differentiation between the two, which is seldom done. Thus the human factors ("charisma" in the secular sense) are sometimes hailed as "spiritual gifts" when they are nothing of the kind. We must not confuse the "cosmetic" and the "charismatic."

But even worse, true charismatic gifts and abilities can be unrecognized because people are looking for the secular "charisma," which may be nonexistent. Thus, some of God's servants can be neglected and rejected, and God's Word not heeded and his gifts not received because the personalities themselves are not attractive enough. So a superficial judgment is passed on people who are genuinely anointed with the Holy Spirit, and their gifts are squandered by the Church.

If we study the Corinthian correspondence, we can see that this was one of the main issues about which the Apostle Paul wrote. There were those in the Church in Corinth who, no doubt, said that Paul lacked "charisma." They apparently said of Paul that "his letters are weighty and strong, but his personal presence is unimpressive, and his speech contemptible" (2 Corinthians 10:10, NASB). In other words, "He's a writer, but he's no speaker, and he has a weak personality." Now they were probably correct, and Paul makes no attempt to deny what they were saying. But where they went wrong was that they dismissed Paul's spiritual authority and gifts because of the absence of those natural but spectacular human gifts they were looking for in him. One fears that many charismatics make the same mistake.

Thus, shallow and unhelpful (even unfruitful) ministries are accepted because they are exciting and humanly attractive, while some of the deeper and more beneficial ministries are ignored or even rejected. Here the "star system" actually quenches the Holy Spirit and deceives Christians. The charismatic renewal has also had its share of frauds and quacks, and thousands have been taken in because, unlike God, they have judged by the outward appearance rather than the heart. If the standards that many charismatics adopt had been adopted in Bible times, David would never have become king and Paul would never have been an apostle. One wonders how much talent has been missed or misunderstood because of this outlook.

God does use personality. He doesn't want colorless, spineless followers. But Christians all too frequently use the same criteria to assess a charismatic personality as they would a TV star. To do so is to deny the work of the Holy Spirit and to base one's faith on mere human factors. The charismatic renewal could do with a few less prima donnas (of both sexes).

DEMON-ADDICTS
(See Appendix A, pp. 119-121; Appendix B, pp. 136, 137.)

The charismatic renewal has had its fill of demon-chasers. In some ways, this has been one of the most harmful areas of the renewal. There have been scandalous examples where the so-called ministry of deliverance has actually caused deaths, with resulting worldwide publicity. In Canada the charismatic renewal received a sickening setback in the 1960's when a woman died in Toronto after a prolonged exorcism during which time she went without normal medication. In the 1970's in Barnsley, England, a man violently murdered his wife after some all-night exorcism sessions.

To quote these two examples shows the dangers of this ministry when things get out-of-hand. They need to be weighed with the fact that there have been thousands of successful exorcisms, and the publicity which attended these two cases was altogether out of proportion when compared with the high success rate in most parts of the world.

There have been several factors which have encouraged the widespread increase of this ministry over the past twenty years. In the first place, there has been an enormous increase in the kind of practices from which people need deliverance. Black magic, spiritualism, the occult, and a host of other practices have been much on the increase as many in our materialistic age seek for "spiritual" experience without being prepared to come to Jesus Christ. Fringe groups and sects have been on the increase everywhere. At the same time, people have turned to charismatics in search of freedom from the effects of these false cults and religions.

But secondly, there has been an increase, through the influence of the charismatic renewal, of Christians who have come to believe in the reality of spiritual power—good and bad. These Christians have gone back to the New Testament and seen in it the way of deliverance. They have discovered that the power of Jesus' name is as effective today as it obviously was then. Much the same kinds of things happen today as did when Jesus and the early Christians ministered to people nearly 2,000 years ago.

So the number of people believing in exorcism has grown at the same time as the number of people who have needed to be exorcised. Some would call this a happy coincidence, even a divine coincidence.

But all has not been well. Again "hot-dog" Christianity has come to the fore. Just as there have been those who have used the leg lengthening ministry for just about everyone, so that it has become for them the answer to many physical disabilities, so others have used exorcism. Thus, many moral defects have been diagnosed as caused by "demons" of one kind or another, as have physical and psychological illnesses. Claims have been made that sexual perversions and practices such as masturbation are caused by Satan, and exorcism delivers people from them. Depression, psychotic illnesses (particularly schizophrenia), and other mental illnesses are the work of demons. Exorcism is the answer.

Spiritual problems are called the result of demonic activity. "If you don't want to pray or read the Bible, you have a demon," people were told. Even the slightest and most momentary contact with spiritualism means you are in bondage. Your release can only come through exorcism. Thus thousands upon thousands of evil spirits have been expelled, but the pastoral effects have been at times disastrous. Momentary elation at a supposed "cure" has led to depressing side effects—especially when the same problems soon reappeared. These ideas encourage a quick solution to all life's problems. Human factors are discounted. The devil is blamed for almost everything and given more credit for evil than he is due. Fear and despondency often result.

I am convinced that the main reason for this exaggerated demonology is faulty theology. If one views the world as almost solely in the hands of either God or Satan, then most things that are not obviously divine and good can be blamed on satanic power through demons. This is sometimes called "dualism." It either leaves out of account most human factors or seriously discounts them. It looks unfavorably on scientific studies, particularly in the field of the behavioral sciences. Its arch-enemy is psychology. While it does simplify the approach to cause and effect, it is wide open to the criticism of being simplistic. I guess we all know those Christians who attribute everything that is "good" to God *directly,* and all evil and misfortune directly to Satan. Human factors are left almost totally out of account.

A balanced study of the New Testament reveals that the apostles didn't see things quite like this. They were in no doubt that the major problem they had to face was human sin, not evil spirits. They were aware of Satan's power and warned the early churches about it. But the majority of pastoral problems the early Christians faced were not directly attributable to evil spirits, but rather to human factors such as pride, lust, jealousy, and gluttony.

It is true that Satan might well capitalize on human weakness. But the answer in most cases lies in the area of the confession of sin, rather than in casting out spirits. And there is no reason to believe that our times in this respect are any different from those of the first century.

But this is not to deny that much real gain has come from the rediscovery of the so-called ministry of deliverance in recent years. And there is evidence to show that some of the more extravagant ministries are more balanced and controlled now than they have been in the past.

Having taken part in this ministry myself, and having seen men and women gloriously delivered from the power of Satan, I can vouch for its effectiveness. I have also written about it and have been encouraged by the letters I have received telling me how useful they have found the book *Spiritual Warfare*.[31] But this is all the more reason for us to safeguard the correct ministry from the abuses which all too easily arise.

DEEP WATER?
(See Appendix A, pp. 115, 116.)

For many Christians the water used in baptism must be deep enough to immerse the candidate. The issue of water baptism has been controversial from the very beginning of the charismatic renewal. The reasons for this are not hard to discover. A large number of Christians who had been baptized as children and who, for the most part, had received practically no sound instruction about their baptism were suddenly confronted for the very first time with the fellowship and teaching of those who believed differently.

The warmth of charismatic fellowship was all that was needed to complete the capture of hosts of Anglicans, Roman Catholics, and Presbyterians and to bring them as candidates to the waters of baptism by total immersion. Because these people were in a time of great spiritual experience when they were confronted with the arguments of those who believe that child baptism is no baptism at all, they were extremely vulnerable to such arguments. Their faith and trust in Jesus Christ had been weak, or in some cases nonexistent, before. It was, therefore, natural that they should wish to witness openly to this new life, and immersion baptism gave them a golden opportunity to do this.

But for some this became "deep water" indeed. A minister of the Swedish State Church (Lutheran) was secretly baptized by immersion, but the secret leaked out. The news reached the ears of his own bishop, who promptly sacked him. The minister appealed to the Minister of Religion, who equally promptly reinstated him. This, of course, raises as many questions about the nature of authority as it does about baptism, but it gives an indication of the seriousness of what some would call "rebaptism." The Roman Catholics treat the matter much more seriously than Anglicans. Some churches even excommunicate those who have a rebaptism. Both the Lutheran Church in Denmark and the Church of South India, for example, regard rebaptism as a very serious offense.

This is not the place to go into the tortuous arguments for and against the various practices. In some respects we are back in the realm of hermeneutics. Many of those who believe in adult baptism by immersion hold the view that we are only to practice what was practiced in the New Testament. Thus, since there are no definite cases of the baptism of children in the New Testament, we should not baptize them today. But most of those who practice infant baptism interpret the New Testament differently. Since, so they would say, there is no prohibition of infant baptism, we are free to practice it, provided it is consistent with the rest of New Testament theology. I would myself take this position, believing that infant baptism is consistent with covenant theology and probably was a natural development from the normal practice of adult baptism in the first century.

But both sides have little to go on, and the arguments hinge on principles of interpretation rather than actual texts, with a lot of cultural influences thrown in. For instance, the excessively individual approach to salvation of Protestant theology would more naturally lead one to a Baptist view of baptism than a Catholic one. But as the tide turns and Christians begin to see things more corporately (as I believe the New Testament does), this opens the way more clearly in the direction of accepting the baptism of the children of Christian parents.

Unfortunately, many have mistakenly thought that there

were no scriptural arguments for the baptism of children. Although there is no definite reference in the New Testament of a child being baptized, it is possible to construct a scriptural argument for the practice on the basis of the nature of baptism itself. Our friends whose practice of baptism is different from ours may well disagree with the arguments. But to say point-blank that infant baptism is "unscriptural" is an unfortunate misrepresentation.

But there are pastoral considerations also in this matter. Baptism cannot be isolated from the Church, for Christian baptism is baptism into the Body of Christ (1 Corinthians 12:13). In the early days of the charismatic renewal, a great deal of pastoral harm was done when large numbers of "sheep" were baptized by "shepherds" who were strangers to them. Often this was done without prior consultation with their own "shepherds." It may have made theological sense, but it certainly didn't make pastoral sense. It is unlikely that the New Testament Church would normally have permitted baptisms except in the context of the local church. Certainly as things developed, baptismal discipline got stronger and stronger.

However, all the indications at the moment point to a much more responsible attitude to the pastoral implications of baptism, or rebaptism as some of us would have to call it. One of the happy results of the so-called discipleship controversy, which hit the United States in 1975, has been that many more charismatic leaders are now taking the Church more seriously and are adopting a more disciplined approach to pastoral structures. Men are more sensitive now in pastoral situations when they are teaching men and women from other churches.

Certainly the large number of people who have been rebaptized has not helped the charismatic renewal in its relationship to those churches which accept paedo-baptism and frown on rebaptism. In some areas it has proved a serious barrier. But the new sensitivity of many is helping to overcome the suspicions and fears that have arisen.

DISCIPLESHIP AND ALL THAT
(See Appendix C, page 141.)

Far and away the most disturbing controversy to hit the charismatic movement has been that of discipleship. The bombshell hit the American scene in 1975.

The effect of what happens in the United States nearly always reaches the rest of the world within a comparatively short time. But to be forewarned is to be forearmed, and most of the charismatic world outside the United States had sufficient warning to avoid the worst features of this affair. Besides, the situation in most of these countries is different from that of the United States, so that it is highly unlikely that the same problems would arise. Nevertheless, the discipleship earthquake had its epicenter in the United States, and the shock waves passed around the world.

In North America by 1975 the charismatic movement had resolved itself into four fairly clearly defined streams. The first stream is that of the classical Pentecostals, the oldest and most obviously structured. The second could be called the Protestant charismatics; by 1975 most of the major denominational churches in the United States had their own charismatic organization. The aim of this stream was to work for renewal in their own churches. The third stream is that of the Roman Catholic renewal, which by 1975 was highly and skillfully organized. The fourth stream is nondenominational, consisting of two main groupings: the independent churches (such as the Melodyland setup in Anaheim, California) and the Christian Growth Ministries of Fort Lauderdale, Florida. The Full Gospel Businessmen's Fellowship International (FGBMFI), although itself not constituting a distinctive stream, has over the years influenced or been influenced by all four streams to some extent.

In 1975, there was a violent confrontation within the nondenominational scene, with some Protestant and classical Pentecostals also involved. The Roman Catholics and most of the Protestants were unaffected. This was no surprise to many people. Charismatic empire building has been going on for many years. It didn't need much to upset the apple cart.

The issue of discipleship was the catalyst. Charismatics openly denounced each other. Christian TV promoter and host Pat Robertson used the media to condemn the CGM. The FGBMFI blackballed them. Vituperation spread across the continent. It became so serious by August that the leaders of the four streams met in Minneapolis. This produced heated, angry exchanges.

The buildup seems to have been this: In 1974 the CGM held a conference for "shepherds" at Montreat, North Carolina. One of the main speakers was Juan Carlos Ortiz, and his talks have been published verbatim in the book *Call to Discipleship*.[32] It was some of Ortiz's teaching, adopted and expanded by the CGM, that sparked off the 1975 confrontation.

In September 1975 the second "shepherds" conference was held in Kansas City. *Logos Journal*, which normally gives favorable coverage to such events, slashed this conference in harsh and sarcastic language, although it was later to apologize for this report. *New Wine*, the organ of the CGM, regarded this conference as a turning point. The issue was already quite inflammable.

But we need to dig deeper to discover the real reasons for this confrontation. Someone has defined cancer as "exuberant growth without relationship to order." This could also pass as a description of some aspects of the charismatic renewal in America. The renewal has produced thousands of nomadic Christians, or sheep without shepherds, and there has been little thought for order and authority. Many have chosen spiritual anarchy, and the casualties have been numerous.

It was this kind of situation that prompted the CGM to bring a new emphasis on shepherding, discipling, and authority. So far so good, and most would say "about time too." At first sight the Roman Catholics and the CGM make strange bedfellows.

But they were *both* stressing the same thing, and there was no doubt that some of the strongest opposition came from those who most needed to hear the message about authority.

On the other hand, one has to remember that whereas the Roman Catholics were concerned largely with para-church structures, the CGM was concerned mainly with churches and regarded these principles as mandatory on all Christians. The crunch came when it was discovered that CGM was distinguishing between ecclesiastical (lip-service) authority and spiritual (the real thing) authority. They were now "discipling" members of other churches and claiming spiritual authority over people who might live hundreds of miles away. And when this was known to involve funds bypassing an individual's church and going to the "shepherds," the fat was in the fire.

In the clearer light of day and looking at the thing through British eyes, where the impact was much less and the damage comparatively small, a number of interesting observations can be made.

In some ways we can see the troubles of 1975-76 as a most important example of how Christians should handle controversy. Christians are regretfully, with few exceptions, bad controversialists. Over the centuries we have seen them adopting two typical positions. There is the defensive position in which both sides dig in and totally ignore each other. We might call this approach "the ostrich approach," for that ungainly animal habitually hides its head in the sand when threatened with danger. Here no personal approach is made. Both sides pretend that the other side does not exist.

Then there is the offensive position. We might call this "the artillery approach." It is really a variation of the first, for the cause of both is the same: the fear of being proved wrong and having to admit it, and the fear of being moved from a secure and well-established position. It is similar to the first in that personal encounter is not in view. The antagonists still remain in carefully prepared defensive positions. But instead of ignoring each other, they hurl shells at one another. Books are written disclosing the "errors" of the enemy. Resolutions are passed and public statements made.

Certainly in the early stages there were some who followed the "ostrich" approach and others who fired their guns at one another. That was a natural consequence of the fear generated by the dispute. But in a remarkably short time and at considerable trouble and expense, the leaders were confronting one another "eyeball to eyeball." A hastily organized Minneapolis meeting in 1975 decided very little. A great deal of anger was expressed. But the foundations were laid for a future settlement which, even if it did not satisfy everyone, not only brought peace where there had been serious controversy, but in the final analysis achieved a far higher level of unity and understanding than had been there before. The ultimate fruit of this was the famous Kansas City Conference of July 1977, when those who had formerly been so deeply at odds with each other shared leadership and spoke on the same platform.

Of course, not all charismatic groups have buried the hatchet. There are some who still are either acting as ostriches or artillerymen. But the moment when, some predicted, the charismatic renewal would end, and when America was within sight of bringing a new denomination to birth, actually brought about a new and deeper unity and commitment than had been known before.

How was this made possible? Writing as an outsider I would pinpoint a few important aspects. The first is the commendable restraint of the CGM leaders. It is true that initially their unbridled enthusiasm for the concept of "discipleship" and their access to the media meant that the Christian world had to face a highly controversial issue without any warning. But even here a public apology was made by the Christian Growth Ministries in 1976 regretting "controversy and problems" that had resulted from their discipleship teaching. They pledged themselves to correct such abuses and misunderstandings wherever possible.

How often do Christian bodies these days make public

apologies to one another? But when the brickbats were flying, the CGM leaders did not retaliate but held their fire, defending themselves only when able to do so face-to-face with their critics. This helped to cool the air.

Another important aspect was the maturity of leadership, and here the Roman Catholics played a strategic part. Already alongside the CGM leadership, they were able to command the respect of both "sides" in the dispute, and to interpret the significance of what was happening. They saw that beneath the superficial (and there was plenty of that to confuse everyone), there were principles at stake which were vital to the future health of the renewal.

Gradually there emerged a consensus of opinion that the days when "everyone did that which was right in their own eyes" had passed, that leaders needed to submit themselves to one another, that sheep needed shepherds, and that some basic understanding of "authority" was essential if further progress was going to be made.

But undergirding it all was a burning desire for unity. They were convinced that because they had already come a long way along similar paths and that the things that united them were far greater than the things that divided, they somehow or other had to find the Holy Spirit's answer. They were now prepared, at personal inconvenience, to jet halfway across the United States in search of that unity.

A workable solution began to be formulated on Dec. 16-17, 1975, when a group of leaders met in Ann Arbor, Michigan "for theological and pastoral evaluation of the current controversy over discipleship and shepherding." A real measure of understanding was reached and a "committed relationship" expressed toward one another.

The report of this meeting was then brought to the larger conference held March 8-12, 1976, in Oklahoma City. This conference accepted the Ann Arbor report, and received and commended the apology from the CGM teachers. It also called for an end to public attacks and malicious gossip, and adopted a statement of ethics as well as setting up a "Charismatic

Concerns Committee" to plan future conferences and help deal with any other issues which might arise in the future. The full report of these meetings can be found in Appendix C.

One is only left to wonder what would have happened if other Christian controversies had been dealt with in a similar fashion. What if Luther had drunk a good pint of German beer with the papal nuncio? Or if John Wesley had been invited to share his views with a group of Anglican bishops? Or if the early Pentecostals had been invited to "talk things over" with other leaders? Or if the early fundamentalists had gone off for a week of prayer and fasting with their liberal "enemies"? It makes one think.

EIGHT
AS OTHERS
SEE US

It is often good for us to see ourselves "as others see us." During the winter of 1977-78 there were two very fascinating examples of this which bear on our subject.

The first was a report on a book published by the Soviet Academy of Sciences and circulated to all universities and libraries in the Soviet Union, arguing that the Church of England is now a dangerous threat to Communist ideology. That might be news indeed to those cynics who would not regard the Church of England as a threat to anything or anyone very much. The author of the book, Yan Yanovitch Veysh, is worried about three particular aspects of the Church of England.

The first is the eclectic nature of Anglicanism, which enables it to play a "unique role" in the worldwide ecumenical movement. The second is its long established and friendly relationship to the Orthodox Church, particularly in Russia itself. And the third is the intellectual caliber of its leadership. The present Archbishop of Canterbury, Dr. Donald Coggan, is singled out as a dangerous man because it is thought (rightly it would seem) that under him the Church of England will pursue the ecumenical cause still more assiduously.

Whatever this may say about the Anglican Church—which

97

does have a unique bridge-building character about it since it contains within its traditions Catholic, evangelical, and charismatic traits—it does say a lot about Christian unity, which is the theme of this book. It reveals, contrary to much popular thinking and writing, that Communist thinkers regard the ecumenical movement as a formidable danger to its own ideology. It sees Christian unity, in other words, as something to be delayed and discouraged. It fears a united Christendom more than some Christians desire it.

Some Christians have regarded the World Council of Churches as almost a secret branch of the KGB. (It is worth mentioning that the Communist world likewise has sometimes smeared American evangelical and charismatic leaders as agents of the CIA.) Whatever way we look at the accusations against the WCC, at least we learn from the Russian book that Communists regard the WCC as a target worthy of their attention, so dangerous do they regard the quest for Christian unity.

Yan Yanovitch Veysh is right here. The kind of unity that this book advocates (with every other kind of Christian unity) would give new power and acceptability to the Christian gospel. The more the prayer of Jesus Christ for unity (John 17) is answered, the more will he be glorified and seen. Our present disunity is a perpetual stumbling block for the world. The Russian book simply underlines the urgency of pursuing every reasonable course to promote greater Christian unity.

The second example of "how others see us" is the December 26, 1977, *Time* magazine. The issue's major feature (including the front cover) was on "The Evangelicals—New Empire of Faith," calling them "the fastest-growing religious movement in the U.S. today." The headline for the cover story was: "Back to That Old-time Religion." But the intriguing feature of the whole issue, which confirms a great deal of what this book is about, is that the high-powered team of top-ranking journalists lumped together without any attempt at delineation the evangelicals and the charismatics as if they belonged together and were part of the same show. Thus, photos of Billy Graham and Oral Roberts, Bill Bright and Pat Robertson were placed in juxtaposition. A leading charismatic parish in the Episcopal Church (St. Paul's Church, Darien, Connecticut) was quoted as a new example of evangelical growth.

In other words, professional journalists could see nothing of importance to delineate between evangelicalism and the comparatively new thrust of the charismatics. So far as they were concerned, they were writing about the same thing—a burgeoning movement described by Rice University sociologist William Martin as "the most active and vital aspect of American religion today." The *Time* reporters commented, "He is almost certainly right."

But whether it is "back to that old-time religion" or not is another matter. There may be comparable features, but one wonders whether the Holy Spirit ever actively endorses something that is "going back." Rather, one should see it as part of the forward march of God's pilgrim people in our day.

For some people, the most difficult aspect of this book to accept will undoubtedly be that involving the Roman Catholic world. I do not have in mind those whose thinking on the subject could be described as preposterously prejudiced, those whose minds were made up, it would seem, by their ancestors centuries ago. But I am thinking of those who when confronted with the Roman Catholic corridors of power can honestly see no light on the road to Christian unity. One can sympathize with such a position.

"Officially" objectionable Catholic doctrines and Rome's stance on Christian unity does not seem to have changed. Even Vatican II's warmer attitudes toward so-called "separated brethren" has not always been reflected in the behavior and statements of Vatican officials since the Council ended. When the Roman Catholic charismatic renewal held its International Conference in Rome in 1975, the organizers acted with considerable caution. No Protestants were allowed on the platform throughout the conference, and none were invited as speakers.

But it may be noted that officials in Rome itself were almost as cool toward their own Catholics as the conference was toward Protestants. Pope Paul VI's warm speech on the Monday in St Peter's Basilica seemed to express his personal viewpoint rather than that of the Curia. The impression often given is that Rome's position is as intransigent as ever.

One of the most abrasive points of controversy is that which surrounds intercommunion. It flared up in England in 1978 when Dr Donald Coggan, the Anglican Archbishop of Canterbury, in an address in the Roman Catholic Westminster Cathedral in London, pleaded strongly for immediate intercommunion between Roman Catholics and Protestants. He had expressed the same sentiments in his personal audience with Pope Paul VI in 1977. Shortly after Dr. Coggan's address, his counterpart, Cardinal Hume, had an opportunity to reply when addressing the General Synod of the Church of England. Predictably, the answer was "no."

The controversy over intercommunion sparked off much correspondence in *The Times*, England's leading national newspaper Dr. Mervyn Stockwood, the Bishop of Southwark, wrote on February 9, "Nobody could question his [Cardinal Hume's] deep sincerity and his utter dedication, but I said to myself, 'He's living on an oasis in an ecclesiastical cloud-cuckoo land which is thousands of miles behind the frontiers of reality.' Meanwhile Christians of all denominations, who are looking up to be fed, will leave their pastors to their fruitless arguments and will vote with their feet. They have walked along the road to Emmaus long enough. It's time to break bread together." Dr. Stockwood was reiterating Dr. Coggan's plain statement of fact that the rules are being broken by so many Christians that the "reasoning" behind such rules is no longer seen.

Now, the reason I've introduced the matter of intercommunion is because it is a very good example of two different worlds which are uncomfortably coexisting at the present time in Roman Catholicism. There is the world of officialdom, sticking rigidly to the rule book. And there is what could be described as "underground ecumenism," a totally different world in which some of these rules are being completely ignored. In George Bernard Shaw's play *St. Joan*, Robert (who is the law-abiding conservative) turns to Poulengey and says, "What! You are as mad as she [Joan] is." Poulengey answers, "We want a few mad people now. See where the sane ones have landed us!"

Underground ecumenism may seem to some the product of madness and a dangerous ecclesiastical aberration. But to others, it seems a work of the Holy Spirit. The "sane" ecumenists and experts on canon law have got us nowhere very much; perhaps the "insane" will achieve something where the others have failed.

Enough said. It is underground ecumenism that this book is mostly about. One is not wanting evangelicals and charismatics to see unity solely in terms of "official ecumenism." There is a place for that too. But chiefly we need to see that a new day has dawned which makes possible ecumenical advance on a scale hitherto never seen before, without having to resort to church officialdom. While one door seems to be still securely locked and bolted, the back door is wide open; so why wait any longer?

ROMAN CATHOLIC PROBLEMS

The Roman Catholic Church has traveled a long way since the days when it was almost universally regarded by evangelicals as synonymous with the "great whore of Babylon" of the Apocalypse. It is not rare these days to be "surprised by the Holy Spirit." But one of these surprises for me was the ease with which I could sit down at a table with Roman Catholics *who had their Bibles open along with mine.*

At times of controversy, I have sometimes suspected that some Christians want to "catch you out" and "expose you," even to distort your arguments for their own ends. But in five years of dialogue with Roman Catholics, I have always found them easy to share with. The reason is simple: they seem to have a love for the truth and a thirst to discover it. They were always insistent that those with whom they seemed to disagree be able to express those disagreements as perfectly as possible. No attempts were made to gloss over differences when they occurred. But I have found Catholics generous toward those who disagreed with them, who in this particular dialogue were inferior to them in theological competence. *But one was never made to feel inferior.* Every Roman Catholic participant acted with considerable courtesy to their opposite numbers.

I hope in saying all this that I may be helping to defuse the fears of many evangelical and charismatic Christians at entering into discussions and sharing biblically with Roman Catholics. I'm not here thinking only of official dialogue, but of the more simple meetings which most of us are able to take part in. I'm sure there are obtuse and even flagrantly dishonest Roman Catholics, just as there are evangelicals and charismatics of the same ilk. But what I am saying is that our past suspicions that such characteristics are normally to be expected of Roman Catholics are totally groundless.

One question that is frequently asked is how renewed Roman Catholics can possibly stay in a Church which teaches so much that is false. One obvious rejoinder would be: how can the rest of the Roman Catholic Church be renewed if those who experience the fullness of God's Spirit leave the Church and join another? But we need to look at the question more deeply than that.

It is difficult for many evangelicals to understand Roman Catholicism at this point. Evangelicalism has usually tended to have a strictly observed doctrinal standard. In other words, it has been "confessional." This has been both a strength and weakness through the centuries. It has meant there has been a solidarity of witness within the particular Church or denomination. But its greatest weakness has been its tendency to split on doctrinal issues. The more narrowly doctrines have been defined, the more this has led to schismatic movements which in the end have formed new denominations. This can be particularly seen in the United States, and the more "modern" the Church, the more open it seems to be toward division or separation.

Roman Catholics, however, have maintained a remarkable

unity through the centuries. A contemporary example of this has been the ferment caused by Vatican II, from which the Church has still not recovered. It has revealed just how many different opinions there are in the Church on a whole range of issues from papal infallibility to birth control, and from the charismatic renewal to Hans Küng. The unity at times seems extremely frail, but there is unity.

I think the main reason for this is the flexible attitude of the Church toward truth. This is not to say Catholics are careless in regard to the truth or that they are two-faced about it. This flexibility seems to spring from a humble attitude toward the truth which eschews arrogant claims to possess it, and a reticence toward the concretization of that truth in the weakness of verbal forms. Words are a powerful way of expressing oneself, but they have a fatal tendency to be both misunderstood and to change their meaning, and the pace of change is forever increasing.

I remember the first time I flew in a Boeing 707 and saw its wings and engine pods moving up and down. I was alarmed and thought the worst. But it makes aerodynamic sense. Wings and engines have to adjust to high turbulence and other stress factors or they would break to pieces in midair. So it would seem the Roman Catholic Church is not as immovable as some assert, at least toward its own members. But one is tempted to add: if only the same Church would be as flexible toward its separated brethren as it is toward its own.

It is because of this attitude to truth that Roman Catholics are able to accept change, when it looks as if the whole thing has been doctrinally tied up for centuries. You can call it casuistry if you like. But the important thing here is to understand it, not pass judgment on it. And it is this kind of approach that makes it possible for charismatics to remain in the Roman Catholic Church and work for its renewal and reformation.

The strange ambivalence which is so common in the Roman Catholic attitude to its teaching is often hard to understand, especially in the light of the Church's hard line on those who have tended to expose its problem areas, especially since

Vatican II. But we need to recognize that this is one thing, a love for the truth is another, and somehow Roman Catholics are able to juggle the two.

OUR APPROACH TO UNITY

There are various ways of approaching Christian unity. There is the painstaking "round-the-conference-table" approach, with open Bibles, thrashing out the doctrinal and historical differences such as the infallibility of the Pope, transubstantiation, the nature of priesthood, the authority of the Church compared with Scripture, and Mariology, to mention some of the major areas of disagreement. This needs to be done and should not be neglected or shirked. But it is not the *only* approach, nor may it even be the most important.

The charismatic renewal's remarkable invasion of the Roman Catholic Church, and the ecumenism which has resulted, should have convinced even the most skeptical that there is what we have called elsewhere "underground ecumenism." It is not "underground" in the sense that it is hidden or forbidden, but because it is unofficial and spontaneous.

Roman Catholics and Protestants have found each other "in the Holy Spirit" and "in Jesus Christ." They have met each other, not at the point of strength, but that of shared human weakness. They have come together in liturgical freedom and joy. In singing together they have melted into a new oneness, which is hard to separate out again.

They have found that they have had to share together at the point of ignorance also. They have both come into new freedom in the Holy Spirit and the experience of fresh gifts and ministries at a time when neither the Roman Catholic Church nor the Protestant churches have known too much about them. They have had, therefore, to learn together what it means to be a charismatic Christian in the twentieth century.

Only at the Lord's Table have they faltered, and even here unofficial (and even sometimes officially sanctioned) joint Communion services or Masses have been held. The prevailing mood of charismatic Christians, both Roman Catholic and Protestant, is that to take Communion together and to receive each other at such services is right in God's sight, even if it is prohibited by the official Church.

We have mentioned doctrinal unity and unity in the Spirit. There is also human unity—the unity which springs from our sharing the same humanity, which through the incarnation and death of Christ has been sanctified. We meet each other as human beings, and our essential humanity is not changed, however radical may be the experience we have of the Holy Spirit. This is often forgotten when we are engaged in what we deem to be "spiritual" ecumenism, but we neglect it at our peril. How seldom in ordinary ecumenical circles does the crucial question of forgiveness come up. Yet how important it is in all human relationships.

Just because it is official ecumenical business does not mean to say that we cease to be human. And could it not be that some of the theological knots which need untying are really the result of personal difficulties, and so should be dealt with at the personal level? Could it not be also that theological opinions are sometimes formed not only through the influence of our minds, but also through our feelings and our personal relationships?

Certainly in the areas we have been discussing there is much forgiving to be done. Charismatics have split evangelical churches. Evangelicals have unfairly attacked charismatics. Roman Catholics have denigrated other churches and persecuted evangelicals. Evangelicals have campaigned against Roman Catholics and separated themselves from them. We have all been at fault, and forgiveness should not be overlooked. There can be no true reconciliation without it, and we shall only be able to travel down the road to unity with it.

I was a witness of a remarkable example of this in Sydney, Australia, in 1977. In January of that year, a large conference was held in the University of New South Wales with the evening meetings in Sydney's largest auditorium, the Hordern Pavilion, next to the famous Sydney cricket ground. It was the first conference of its kind ever to be held in Australia. The Roman Catholics had their own conference first, and then both Catholics and Protestants met for a united conference, which was also supported by some of the classical Pentecostals.

It needs to be remembered that only a few years before this, the American Pentecostal evangelist Oral Roberts (who is now a Methodist) was literally chased out of Australia, after riots and threats to destroy his big tent in Melbourne. Sydney is a bastion of evangelical orthodoxy also. In the Anglican diocese, there is only one nonevangelical parish and anti-Catholic feeling still runs high. When Pope Paul VI visited Sydney, the Anglican Archbishop (Dr. Marcus Loane) refused to attend a service in the Roman Catholic Cathedral. This is the background to the events on the Thursday evening of the conference.

This particular evening had been billed as a "healing service." It certainly turned out that way, although not as most people present expected. The speakers were Francis MacNutt from St. Louis, Missouri, and Tommy Tyson from North Carolina. Francis is a Dominican and Tommy a Methodist. Both spoke about the power of forgiveness, and over 5,000 listened quietly as Francis and Tommy led everyone in an act of confession and forgiveness. Francis confessed Catholic sin toward Protestants and asked for forgiveness. Tommy confessed the sins that Protestants had committed against Catholics. Something unusual began to happen. The healing power of Christ was released. I saw that night a microcosm of the work of the Spirit of unity. Bridges were being built across yawning chasms, and people filed slowly over them toward each other and common ground. There was much weeping that night. We felt the pain of separation. We felt the hurts in the Body of Christ, the wounds that mar the beauty of the Bride of Christ, but wounds that were being healed before our very eyes.

I know that one must not build too much on a single incident. Conferences inevitably are unreal events, and the real thing happens back home when the euphoria that conferences generate has worn off. But sometimes God does use a single event to teach an important lesson. The Chinese proverb is true: the longest journey begins with the first step. This may well have been for many the first faltering step toward "separated brethren." The journey ahead may be long and arduous, but at least it has commenced.

One would not want for a moment to minimize the real difficulties that face the reconciliation of the "three sisters" in the family of God, and that goes for others in the family also. The road ahead is hard, and there are many obstacles to progress. This book is a plea that the journey which some have started should be completed whatever the cost; and that those who for one reason or other have never begun should take those first faltering steps.

The penalty for our failure is the continued weakness of the body of Christ on earth, the impairment of its witness in the world, and the delay of the return of its Lord. The prize is the release of new power for the people of God as they unite together, and the hastening of the coming of Christ for the kind of Church he prayed for.

APPENDIX A
FINAL REPORT OF DIALOGUE BETWEEN ROMAN CATHOLICS, PENTECOSTALS, AND CHARISMATICS

Final report of the dialogue between the Secretariat for Promoting Christian Unity of the Roman Catholic Church and leaders of some Pentecostal Churches and participants in the charismatic movement within Protestant and Anglican Churches, 1972-1976.

INTRODUCTION

1. The series of talks described as the Roman Catholic Pentecostal dialogue had its beginning in the contacts made by individual members of the Pentecostal Churches with the Vatican Secretariat for Promoting Christian Unity in 1969 and 1970. With the assistance of Revd. David du Plessis, an international Pentecostal leader, noted figure among Pentecostals, and a guest at the Second Vatican Council and Fr. Kilian McDonnell, OSB, Director of the Institute for Ecumenical and Cultural Research, Collegeville, U.S.A., the initial impulse was clarified and concrete proposals began to emerge.

2. In 1970 the first of two exploratory meetings was held to see if a serious theological discussion between Roman Catholics and Pentecostals on the international level would be

possible. The first gathering was largely an occasion to know one another. At the second meeting in 1971 each side put "hard" questions to the other, a more purposeful conversation resulted, and it became clear that it would be possible to undertake discussions of a more systematic kind.

3. Therefore, later in 1971, a small steering committee with members from both sides worked out a program of topics which could be treated at meetings over a five-year period.

4. The dialogue has a special character. The bilateral conversations which the Roman Catholic Church undertakes with many world communions, e.g. the Anglican Communion, the Lutheran World Federation, etc., are prepared to consider problems concerning Church structures and ecclesiology and have organic unity as a goal or at least envisage some kind of eventual structural unity. This dialogue has not. Before it began it was made clear that its immediate scope was not "to concern itself with the problems of imminent structural union," although of course its object was Christians coming closer together in prayer and common witness. Its purpose has been that "prayer, spirituality and theological reflection be a shared concern at the international level in the form of a dialogue between the Secretariat for Promoting Christian Unity of the Roman Catholic Church and leaders of some Pentecostal Churches and participants in the charismatic movement within Protestant and Anglican Churches."

5. The dialogue has sought "to explore the life and spiritual experience of Christians and the Churches," to give special attention to "the meaning for the Church of fullness of life in the Holy Spirit," attending to "both the experiential and theological dimensions" of that life. "Through such dialogue" those who participate "hope to share in the reality of the mystery of Christ and the Church, to build a united testimony, to indicate in what manner the sharing of truth makes it possible . . . to grow together."

6. Certain areas of doctrinal agreement have been looked at with a view to eliminating mutual misunderstandings. At the same time, there has been no attempt to minimize points of real

divergence. One of these, for example, is the importance given to faith and to experience, and their relation in Christian life.

7. The dialogue has been between the Roman Catholic Church and some Pentecostal Churches. Here, too, there have been special features. On the Roman Catholic side, it has had the usual authorization given by the Secretariat for Promoting Christian Unity to such meetings on an international scale and the participants were appointed officially by their individual Churches (and in several cases are leaders of these Churches), or else came with some kind of approbation of their Churches. Therefore, it has been a dialogue with some Pentecostal Churches and with delegates of others. These are Churches which came into being over the last fifty or sixty years when some Protestant Churches expelled those who made speaking in tongues and other charismatic manifestations an integral part of their spirituality.

8. In addition, there were participants in the charismatic movement who were invited by the Pentecostals. They belong to Anglican or Protestant Churches which already have bilateral dialogues in progress with the Roman Catholic Church. Therefore, it is as participants in the charismatic movement and not primarily as member of their own Churches that they share in the dialogue.

9. It was also pointed out in the beginning that "this dialogue is not directly concerned with the domestic pastoral question of the relationship of the charismatic movement among Catholics to the Catholic Church. The dialogue may help indirectly to clarify this relationship but this is not the direct concern of our deliberations."

10. At the first meeting of the dialogue in Horgen, Switzerland, June 1972, an exegetical approach was taken in order to study "baptism in the Holy Spirit" in the New Testament, its relation to repentance and the process of sanctification and the relation of the charismata to it. At Rome in June 1973 the second meeting was devoted to the historic background of the Pentecostal movement, the relation of baptism in the Holy Spirit to the rites of Christian initiation, and the role of the

Holy Spirit and the gifts of the Spirit in the mystical tradition. The third meeting, held at Schloss Craheim, West Germany, June 1974, focused on the theology of Christian initiation, the nature of sacramental activity, infant and adult baptism. At the fourth meeting held in Venice, May 1975, the areas of public worship (especially eucharistic celebration), the human dimension in the exercise of the spiritual gifts, and discerning of spirits were the main concern. In Rome, May 1976, the final session was devoted to the topic of prayer and praise.

BAPTISM IN THE HOLY SPIRIT

11. In the New Testament the expression "to baptize in the Holy Spirit" (Mark 1:8) is used to express in contrast to the baptism of John (John 1:33) the baptism by Jesus who gives the Spirit to the new eschatological people of God, the Church (Acts 1:5). All men are called to enter into this community through faith in Christ who makes them disciples through baptism and sharers of his Spirit (Acts 2:38, 39).

12. In the Pentecostal movement "being baptized in the Spirit," "being filled with the Holy Spirit," and "receiving the Holy Spirit" are understood as occurring in a decisive experience distinct from conversion whereby the Holy Spirit manifests himself, empowers and transforms one's life, and enlightens one as to the whole reality of the Christian mystery (Acts 2:4; 8:17; 10:44; 19:6).

13. It is the Spirit of Christ which makes a Christian (1 Cor. 12:13) and that life is "Christian" inasmuch as it is under the Spirit and is characterized by openness to his transforming power. The Spirit is sovereignly free, distributing his gifts to whomsoever he wills, whenever and howsoever he wills (1 Cor. 12:11; John 3:7, 8). There is also the human responsibility to seek after what God has promised (1 Cor. 14:1). This full life in the Spirit is growth in Christ (Eph. 4:15, 16) which must be purified continually. On the other hand, due to one's unfaithfulness to the promptings of the Spirit (Gal. 6:7-9; 1 John 3:24) this growth can be arrested. But also new ways open up and new

112

crises occur which could be milestones of progress in the Christian life (2 Cor. 3:17, 18; 2 Cor. 4:8-11).

14. The participants are conscious that during the nineteen centuries other terms have been used to express this experience called "baptism in the Holy Spirit." It is one used today by the Pentecostal movement. Other expressions are "being filled with the Holy Spirit," "receiving the Holy Spirit." These expressions should not be used to exclude traditional understandings of the experience of and faith in the reality of Christian initiation.

15. The Holy Spirit gratuitously manifests himself in signs and charisms for the common good (Mark 16:17-18), working in and through but going beyond the believer's natural ability. There is a great variety of ministries in which the Spirit manifests himself. Without minimizing the importance of these experiences or denying the fruitfulness of these gifts for the Church, the participants wished to lay stronger stress on faith, hope and charity as sure guides in responding to God (1 Cor. 13:13—14:1; 1 Thess. 1:3-5). Precisely out of respect for the Spirit and his gifts it is necessary to discern between true gifts and their counterfeits (1 Thess. 5:22; 1 John 4:1-4). In this discernment process the spiritual authority in the Church has its own specific ministry (1 John 4:6; Acts 20:28-31; 1 Cor. 14:37, 38) because it has special concern for the common good, the unity of the Church and her mission in the world (Rom. 15:17-19; Acts 1:8).

CHRISTIAN INITIATION AND THE GIFTS

16. From the earliest noncanonical texts of the Church there is witness to the celebration of Christian initiation (baptism, laying-on of hands/chrismation, Eucharist) as clearly expressing the request for and the actual reception of the Holy Spirit. The Holy Spirit dwells in all Christians (Rom. 8:9), and not just in those "baptized in the Holy Spirit." The difference between a committed Christian without such a Pentecostal experience and one with such an experience is generally not

only a matter of theological focus, but also that of expanded openness and expectancy with regard to the Holy Spirit and his gifts. Because the Holy Spirit apportions as he wills in freedom and sovereignty, the religious experiences of persons can differ. He blows where he wills (John 3:8). Though the Holy Spirit never ceased manifesting himself throughout the entire history of the Church, the manner of the manifestations has differed according to the times and cultures. However, in the Pentecostal movement, the manifestation of tongues has had, and continues to have, particular importance.

17. During times of spiritual renewal when charismatic elements are more manifest, tensions can arise because of prejudice, lack of mutual understanding and communication. Also, at such times as this the discerning of spirits is more necessary than ever. This necessity should not lead to discernment being misused so as to exclude charismatic manifestations. The true exercise of the charisms takes place in love and leads to a greater fidelity to Christ and his Church. The presence of charismatic gifts is not a sign of spiritual maturity and those who lack experience of such gifts are not considered to be inferior Christians. Love is the context in which all gifts are rightly exercised, love being of a more definitive and primary order than the spiritual gifts (1 Cor. 13). In varying degrees all the charisms are ministries directed to the building up of the community and witness in mission. For this reason mystical experiences, which are more generally directed toward personal communion with God, are distinguished from charismatic experiences which, while including personal communion with God, are directed more to ministerial service.

THE GIVING OF THE SPIRIT
AND CHRISTIAN INITIATION

18. The Holy Spirit, being the agent of regeneration, is given in Christian initiation, not as a commodity but as he who unites us with Christ and the Father in a personal relationship. Being a Christian includes the reception of grace through the Holy

Spirit for one's own sanctification as well as gifts to be ministered to others. In some manner all ministry is a demonstration of the power of the Spirit. It was not agreed whether there is a further imparting of the Spirit with a view to charismatic ministry, or whether baptism in the Holy Spirit is, rather, a kind of release of a certain aspect of the Spirit already given. An inconclusive discussion occurred on the question as to how many impartings of the Spirit there were. Within classical Pentecostalism some hold that through regeneration the Holy Spirit comes into us, and that later in the baptism in the Spirit the Spirit comes upon us and begins to flow from us. Finally, charisms are not personal achievements but are sovereign manifestations of the Holy Spirit.

BAPTISM

19. Baptism involves a passing over from the kingdom of darkness to Christ's kingdom of light, and always includes a communal dimension of being baptized into the one Body of Christ. The implications of this concord were not developed.

20. In regard to baptism, the New Testament reflects the missionary situation of the apostolic generation of the Church and does not clearly indicate what may have happened in the second and following generation of believers.

21. In that missionary situation Christian initiation involved a constellation normally including proclamation of the Gospel, faith, repentance, baptism in water, the receiving of the Spirit. There was disagreement as to the relationship of these items, and the order in which they may or should occur. In both the Pentecostal and Roman Catholic tradition laying-on of hands may be used to express the giving of the Spirit. Immersion is the ideal form which most aptly expresses the significance of baptism. Some, however, regard immersion as essential, others do not.

22. In discussing infant baptism, certain convergences were noted: (a) Sacraments are in no sense magical and are effective only in relationship to faith.

23. (b) God's gift precedes and makes possible human receiving. Even though there was disagreement on the application of this principle, there was accord on the assertion that God's grace operates in advance of our conscious awareness.

24. (c) Where paedobaptism is not practiced and the children of believing parents are presented and dedicated to God, the children are thus brought into the care of the Christian community and enjoy the special protection of the Lord.

25. (d) Where paedobaptism is practiced it is fully meaningful only in the context of the faith of the parents and the community. The parents must undertake to nurture the child in the Christian life, in the expectation that, when he or she grows up, the child will personally live and affirm faith in Christ.

26. Representatives of the charismatic movement in the historic Churches expressed different views on baptism. Some agreed substantially with the Roman Catholic, others with the classical Pentecostal view.

27. Attention was drawn to the pastoral problem of persons baptized in infancy seeking a new experience of baptism by immersion later in life. It was stated that in a few traditions rites have been devised, involving immersion in water in order to afford such an experience. The Roman Catholics felt there were already sufficient opportunities within the existing liturgy for reaffirming one's baptism. Rebaptism in the strict sense of the word is unacceptable to all. Those participants who reject paedobaptism, however, explained that they do not consider as rebaptism the baptism of a believing adult who has received infant baptism. This serious ecumenical problem requires future study.

SCRIPTURE, TRADITION AND DEVELOPMENTS

28. The Church is always subject to sacred scriptures. There was, however, considerable disagreement as to the role of tradition in interpretation of scripture.

29. The Pentecostal and charismatic movements have

brought to the understanding of scripture a new relevance and freshness to confirm the conviction that scripture has a special message, vital to each generation. Moreover, these movements challenge the exegetes to take a new look at the sacred text in the light of the new questions and expectations the movements bring to scripture.

30. It was agreed that every Church has a history, and is inevitably affected by its past. Some developments in that past are good, some are questionable; some are enduring, some are only temporary. A discernment must be made on these developments for the Churches.

CHARISMATIC RENEWAL
IN THE HISTORIC CHURCHES

31. The dialogue considered that in the context of the charismatic movement in the historic Churches there was justification for new groups and communities within the Churches. Though such movements have a legitimate prophetic character, their ultimate purpose is to strengthen the Church, and to participate fully in her life. Therefore, the charismatic movement is not in competition with the Churches, nor is it separate from them. Further, it should recognize the Church authorities. In a word the charismatic renewal is a renewal in the Body of Christ, the Church, and is, therefore, in and of the Church.

PUBLIC WORSHIP

32. Public worship should safeguard a whole composite of elements: spontaneity, freedom, discipline, objectivity. On the Roman Catholic side, it was noted that the new revised liturgy allows for more opportunities for spontaneous prayer and singing at the Eucharist and in the rites of penance. The Pentecostal tradition has come to accept a measure of structure in worship and recognizes the development in its own history toward some liturgy.

33. In the Roman Catholic context the phrase *ex opere operato* was discussed in relation to the celebration of the sacraments. The disquiet of some participants was removed by the explanation of the Roman Catholic doctrine of grace which stresses that the living faith of the recipient of a sacrament is of fundamental importance.

PUBLIC WORSHIP AND THE GIFTS

34. Corporate worship is a focal expression of the worshipper's daily life as he or she speaks to God and to other members of the community in songs of praise and words of thanksgiving (Eph. 5:19, 20; 1 Cor. 14:26). Our Lord is present in the members of his body, manifesting himself in worship by means of a variety of charismatic expressions. He is also present by the power of his Spirit in the Eucharist. The participants recognized that there was a growing understanding of the unity which exists between the formal structure of the eucharistic celebration and the spontaneity of the charismatic gifts. This unity was exemplified by the Pauline relationship between chapters eleven to fourteen of 1 Corinthians.

THE HUMAN ASPECT

35. There exists both a divine and human aspect to all genuinely charismatic phenomena. So far as concerns the human aspect, the phenomena can rightly be subject to psychological, linguistic, sociological, anthropological and other investigations which can provide some understanding of the diverse manifestations of the Holy Spirit. But the spiritual aspect of charismatic phenomena ultimately escapes a purely scientific examination. While there is no essential conflict between science and faith, nevertheless, science has inherent limitations, particularly with regard to the dimensions of faith and spiritual experience.

36. A survey of the scientific literature on speaking in tongues was presented. Another presentation outlined a Jungian psychological evaluation of the phenomenology of the

Holy Spirit. However, neither of these topics was developed adequately in discussion and they await more extended consideration. This could be done in the context of a future treatment of the place of speaking in tongues as an essential factor in the Pentecostal experience.

37. The relationship between science and the exercise of the spiritual gifts, including that of healing, was discussed. Classical Pentecostals, as well as other participants, believe that through the ministry of divine healing can come restoration to sound health. Full agreement was not reached in this matter in view of the importance of the therapeutic disciplines and the participants recommended further in-depth study.

DISCERNMENT OF SPIRITS

(38) The New Testament witnesses to the charism of the discerning of spirits (1 Cor. 12:10) and also to a form of discernment through the testing of the spirits (1 John 4:1) and the proving of the will of God (Rom. 12:2), each exercised in the power of the Spirit. There are different aspects of discernment of spirits which allow for human experience, wisdom and reason as a consequence of growth in the Spirit, while other aspects imply an immediate communication of the Spirit for discernment in a specific situation.

(39) Discernment is essential to authentic ministry. The Pentecostal tradition lays stress on the discerning of spirits in order to find the mind of the Spirit for ministry and public worship. It is also understood as a diagnostic gift which leads to the further manifestation of other charismata for the edification of the Body of Christ and the work of the Gospel. The operation of this gift in dependence upon the Spirit develops both in the believer and community a growth in a mature sensitivity to the Spirit.

(40) Normally, but not absolutely, expectancy is a requisite for the manifestations of the Spirit through human acts on the part of the believer and the community; that is, an openness which nevertheless respects the sovereignty of the Spirit in the

distribution of his gifts. Because of human frailty, group pressure and other factors, it is possible for the believer to be mistaken or misled in his awareness of the Spirit's intention and influence in the believer's acts. It is for this reason that criteria are essential to confirm and authenticate the genuine operation of the Spirit of truth (1 John 4:1-6). These criteria must be based upon the scriptural foundation of the Incarnation, the Lordship of Christ and the building up of his Church. The important element of community criteria involves the common wisdom of a group of believers, walking and living in the Spirit, when, led by those exercising the ministry of discernment, a mature discipline results and the group is capable of discerning the mind of God.

(41) The Roman Catholic tradition understands such community discernment to be exercised by the whole Church of which her leaders receive a special charism for this purpose. All traditions find a confirmatory individual criterion in the extent to which the believer is influenced in his daily life by the Spirit of Christ who produces love, joy, peace, the plenitude of the fruit of the Spirit (Gal. 5:22).

PRAYER AND PRAISE

(42) The relationship between the objective and the subjective aspect of Christian life was raised. Prayer has two main forms: praise and petition. Both have an objective and a subjective aspect.

In the prayer of praise the essential aspect is worship itself, the adoration of the Father in the Spirit and in the truth of Christ (cf. John 4:23-24). One of the expressions of this prayer of praise is the gift of tongues, with joy, enthusiasm, etc.

In the prayer of petition, the believer has always to distinguish between God the giver, and the gift, of God.

(43) Also discussed was the relationship between the word of God and our experience of the Spirit. The Bible must always

be a control and a guide in the Christian experience; but on the other hand, the spiritual experience itself constantly invites us to read the Bible spiritually, in order that it become living water in our Christian life.

(44) We recognize multiple aspects of the total Christian experience which embraces the presence of God (joy, enthusiasm, consolation, etc.) and also the experience of our own sin and the experience of the absence of God, with Christ dying on the cross (Mark 15:34; Phil. 3:10), desolation, aridity and the acceptance of our personal death in Christ as an integral part of the authentic Christian life and also of the true praise of God.

TOPICS FOR FURTHER DISCUSSION
(45) In the course of conversations a number of areas were touched on which are recommended for further study. Among them were the following:

(a) Speaking in tongues as a characteristic aspect of the experience in the Pentecostal movement.

(b) The subjective dispositions relative to the baptism in the Holy Spirit.

(c) The relationship between the faith of the individual and the faith of the community in terms of content.

(d) The relationship between faith and experience.

(e) The psychological dimension of charismatic experience.

(f) An examination of the charismata of healing and the casting out of demons.

(g) The relationship between the sacraments and conscious personal response of God.

(h) The nature of the sacramental event and, in this context, the nature of the Church.

(i) The problem of interpreting scripture.

(j) The ministries and the ministry gifts: their purpose and operation.

(k) The social implications of spiritual renewal.

CHARACTER OF THE FINAL REPORT

(46) The character of the final report compiled by the Steering Committee which has served the dialogue does not represent the official position of the classical Pentecostal Churches, or of the Roman Catholic Church. Rather, it represents the content of the discussions. Though the conclusions are the result of serious study and dialogue by responsible persons, it does not commit any of the Churches or traditions to the theological positions here expressed, but is submitted to them for suitable use and reaction.

It has been the consensus of all participants that the dialogue has been an occasion of mutual enrichment and understanding and offers the promise of a continuing relationship.

APPENDIX B
"GOSPEL AND SPIRIT" JOINT STATEMENT OF ANGLICAN EVANGELICALS AND CHARISMATICS

A joint statement prepared and agreed by a group nominated by the Fountain Trust and the Church of England Evangelical Council and consisting of:

John Baker	Jim Packer
Colin Buchanan	Harold Parks
John Collins	Gavin Reid
Ian Cundy	Tom Smail
Michael Harper	John Stott
Raymond Johnston	Raymond Turvey
Bruce Kaye	Tom Walker
Gordon Landreth	David Watson
Robin Nixon	

BACKGROUND

A group nominated by the Church of England Evangelical Council and the Fountain Trust respectively met together for four valuable day conferences over a period of eighteen months. We are glad that we did so, and acknowledge that our failure to do so earlier may have helped to prolong unnecessary misunderstandings and polarisations.

We do not all see eye to eye on every point, but we thankfully recognise that what unites us is far greater than the matters on which some of us still disagree. We share the same evangelical faith, recognising each other as brothers in Christ and in the gospel, and we desire to remain in fellowship and to build yet stronger relationships of love and trust.

Our task has been to try to articulate widely held and representative attitudes among the so-called 'charismatic' and 'non-charismatic' leaders of Anglican Evangelicalism and to bring both to the bar of Holy Scripture. We have sought to understand each other's views better and to achieve closer harmony and correspondence through examining them all in the light of biblical teaching. We are now issuing this account of our progress, indicating both agreements and disagreements, in the hope that it may help to promote unity where there is discord, and mutual understanding where there has been mistrust.

We have been struck by the fact that in our discussions, differences of view (usually denoted by 'some' and 'others' in the text) have by no means always coincided with our 'charismatic' and 'non-charismatic' identifications.

1. *The charismatic movement and Anglican Evangelicalism*

a) The charismatic movement in the United Kingdom has evangelical roots, but is now both trans-denominational and trans-traditional, and embraces a very wide spectrum of views, attitudes and practices, not all originating from a recognised evangelical 'stable'. Anglican Evangelicalism also embraces a wide spectrum of views and emphases, as one would expect of a movement that has been developing and adapting itself over four centuries. In our exchanges we have tried to bear in mind the complexity of both constituencies and to avoid facile over-simplifications. Readers of this statement will judge how far we have succeeded.

b) We are united in thanking God for the real and obvious deeper acquaintance with Jesus Christ and his saving grace which charismatic renewal has brought to many individuals and the new life and vigour which many churches have come to enjoy as a result. We acknowledge however that with this there have been dangers and sometimes disasters, which have called for some self-criticism.

We rejoice too that renewal of spiritual life is manifestly not confined to 'charismatic' circles and churches, while we share a common sadness that much of the Church, both Evangelical and non-Evangelical, seems as yet to be untouched by true renewal in any form. In the quest for a quickening of the whole Church we believe ourselves substantially to be making common cause.

c) During the past thirty years sections of Anglican Evangelicalism have experienced a notable renewal of concern for the study and teaching of the doctrines of the faith. The main concern of the charismatic renewal, at least until recently, has been experimental rather than theological.

The resulting sense of polarisation and of being threatened at the level of one's priorities, purposes and programmes may not have been justified, but has certainly been a potent cause of both tension and coolness. In our conversations we sought to overcome these inhibitions and build bridgeheads for future fellowship, trust and co-operation, and this we believe we have been enabled to do.

2. *Christian initiation and baptism in the Spirit:*
relating terms and experience

a) All gospel blessings given in Christ. We all agree that every spiritual blessing is given to us by God in and through our Lord Jesus Christ (Eph. 1:3), so that every Christian is, in principle, complete, receiving fullness of life in him (Col. 2:9-10). The Christ whom together we worship is the Jesus of the New Testament, God's Son incarnate who died for our sins, rose again and now lives and reigns. The gift of the Holy Spirit to believers is part of the ministry to them of our crucified, risen and ascended Lord, and the ministry of the Spirit is always to communicate, exalt and bear witness to this glorified Christ.

We thus agree in our understanding of how the ministry of the Spirit is related to the Father and the Son, and in rejecting the idea that in the Spirit we receive something more wonderful than our Saviour, or something apart from him and the fullness of his saving grace.

b) Initiation into Christ. We are all convinced that according to the New Testament Christian initiation, symbolised and sealed by water-baptism, is a unitary work of God with many facets. This work is expressed by a cluster of partly overlapping concepts, including forgiveness, justification, adoption, regeneration, conversion (embracing repentance and faith in Jesus Christ as Lord and Saviour), new creation, death, burial and resurrection in and with Christ, and the giving and reception of the Holy Spirit.

These concepts may be logically separated for consideration in teaching and learning; God's initiatory work is itself apprehended and experienced by different individuals in differing ways and time-scales; and certain aspects of it are in fact times absent in evangelism, teaching, awareness and conscious experience. But essentially the concepts all belong together, since together they express the single full reality of the believer's incorporation into Christ, which leads to assurance of sonship, and power to live and serve in Christ.

We are agreed on the need (i) to avoid trying to stereotype or straitjacket either the work of the Holy Spirit or the experience of individual Christians into a one, two or three-stage experience; (ii) to avoid presenting the work of the Spirit in separation from the work of the Son, since the Son gives the Spirit and the Spirit both witnesses to the Son and forms him in us; and (iii) to present the full range of Christ's salvation and gift for us in all our evangelism and teaching—i.e., to preach a complete, rather than a truncated gospel.

c) Terminology: 'baptism in the Spirit'. We are agreed that every Christian is indwelt by the Holy Spirit (Rom. 8:9). It is impossible for anyone to acknowledge sin, confess Christ, experience new birth, enjoy the Saviour's fellowship, be assured of sonship, grow in holiness, or fulfil any true service or ministry without the Spirit. The Christian life is life in the Spirit. We all thank God for this gift.

In recent years there has been, as we said, a fresh enrichment in many Christians' Spirit-given experience of Christ, and in many cases they have called it 'baptism in the Holy Spirit'. Some of these people have seen their experience as similar to that of the disciples on the day of Pentecost, and other comparable events in Acts. Despite the observable parallels, however, there are problems attaching to the use of this term to describe an experience separated, often by a long period of time, from the person's initial conversion to Christ.

In the first place, this usage suggests that what is sub-normal in the New Testament should be regarded as normal today: that a long interval should elapse between new birth and any conscious realisation or reception of the Spirit's power.

In the second place, the New Testament use of the words 'baptise' and especially 'baptise into' stresses their initiatory content and context, and therefore refers to Christian initiation, rather than to a later enrichment of Christian experience.

However, we see that it may be hard to change a usage which has become very widespread, although we all agree in recognising its dangers. We would all emphasise that it must not be employed in a way which would question the reality of the work of the Spirit in regeneration and the real difference that this brings in experience from the outset. On that we are unanimous.

Some who speak of a post-conversion 'baptism in the Spirit' think of it mainly in terms of an empowering for service similar to the disciples' experience at Pentecost, though all are agreed that we should not isolate this side of the Spirit's work from his other ministries to and in the believer.

Some, stressing the experiential content of the term 'baptism in the Spirit', value it as having played a unique part in awakening Christians out of spiritual lethargy and bondage, and regard it as still having such a role in the future. Others, concentrating rather upon its initiatory implications, prefer to use it only to describe one aspect of new birth.

None of us wishes to deny the possibility or reality of subsequent experiences of the grace of God which have deep and transforming significance. We all affirm that a constant hunger and thirst after God should characterise every Christian, rather than any complacent claim to have 'arrived'. We urge one another and all our fellow-Christians to press on to know the Lord better, and thus to enter into the fullness of our inheritance in Christ (Ph. 3:8-16).

d) Initial evidence of having received the gift of the Spirit. Although speaking in tongues is an initial phenomenon recorded on a number of occasions in connection with receiving the Holy Spirit in the book of Acts, the New Testament will not allow us to make it either the only, or the universal, or an indubitable evidence that this gift has been given. Indeed, we believe it is dangerous to appear to identify the Giver with the presence of any one of his gifts in isolation, however valuable that gift might be in itself.

Nevertheless, it seems clear that the reception of the Spirit by Christians in the New Testament was something experienced, evidenced and often immediately perceived, rather than merely inferred (cf Ac. 19:2, Ga. 3:2).

When we ask what evidence of this reception we might expect, in the light of the New Testament records, the immediate answer must be a new awareness of the love, forgiveness and presence of God as our Father through Jesus Christ who is confessed as Lord, and the joyful spontaneous praise of God (whether in one's own tongue or another), issuing subsequently in a life of righteousness and obedience, and of loving service to God and man, a life which manifests gifts of the Spirit as well as spiritual understanding.

3. Spiritual ethos

a) Emotion and intellect: doctrine and experience. We are aware that there is a real danger of exalting the intellect and understanding at the expense of the emotions. We know too that there is an equal danger of reacting against this into an anti-intellectual and emotionalist form of piety. We wish to assert, against both these extremes, the importance in faith and worship of the whole person.

We believe the mind must be involved in understanding the faith and applying it, and that the emotions, as well as the will, must be involved in our response to the truth and love of God, as well in his worship as in the compassionate service of our fellow men. Both doctrine and experience, word and Spirit, must go together, biblical doctrine testing, interpreting and controlling our experience, and experience fulfilling, incarnating and expressing our beliefs. Only so can we avoid the two extremes of a dead, rigid and barren orthodoxy, or an uncontrolled, unstable and fanatical emotionalism.

b) Worship. We believe that what are seen as characteristic features of 'evangelical' and 'charismatic' worship and spirituality will complement and enrich one another and correct the imbalances in each, although we recognize that in some situations the two so overlap already as to be almost indistinguishable. Many 'charismatic' gatherings would benefit from order, teaching, and some robustly doctrinal 'evangelical' hymns; just as many 'evangelical' services and prayer meetings would benefit from more spontaneity, greater participation, a more relaxed atmosphere, the gentle, loving wonder and praise of some renewal songs, and learning to listen to God in times of prayer and meditation.

c) Faith: passive and active. A different emphasis appears on occasion regarding the exercise of faith in the promises of the blessings offered to us by Christ in the gospel. 'Evangelicals' have sometimes laid all stress on the acceptance of Christ and his forgiveness and salvation at the outset, leading to commitment, and expected God then and thereafter to pour out his blessings in Christ without any necessary appropriating prayers of faith on our part—because it is his way to do more than we ask or think, and to give us many things without our asking. 'Charismatic' Christians, however, are among those who stress the need for the exercise of expectant and appropriating faith in prayer for blessings and gifts God has promised to bestow upon us.

Both emphases can find support in the New Testament, and are complementary rather than mutually exclusive. Faith must both passively rest in the confidence of our Father's general goodness and generosity, trusting his wisdom to supply what we need as he sees it, but also on occasion pray actively and expectantly on the basis of his specific promises to his children and church, to claim their fulfilment as covenanted by him in answer to our prayers.

We all recognise further that sometimes our Father in his wisdom does not answer his children's prayers immediately, in order to teach us patiently and trustingly to wait upon him for his gifts. This saves us from lapsing from a living relationship into any automatic view of prayer, and helps us to trust him to give what we need and ask for in the way and at the time which he knows to be best for us.

4. *Church life, structures and relationships*

a) The body of Christ. According to the New Testament the whole church is a charismatic community in which all are endowed with spiritual gifts (charismata) and are responsible for exercising them for the common good. The charismatic movement has been one of the forces which in recent years have begun healthily to correct an earlier excessive individualism, through recovery of the biblical emphasis upon the body of Christ.

We welcome this, with its corollary of every member being able to play a full part, through the Spirit's equipping, in the church's life, worship, witness and service. We recognize that under God this emphasis has prompted much hard work and patient ministry in the whole field of personal relationships and Christian life in community, and this we all applaud.

b) Structures. If these gains are to be assimilated, traditional ways of worship, ministry and congregational life must be modified and adapted. The doctrine and reality of the body of Christ cannot adequately be expressed through a pattern of ministry dependent chiefly, if not entirely, on one man, nor through exclusive use of a totally rigid 'set' pattern of worship.

Our Anglican heritage at both these points can and should be made flexible, so as to combine with, and contribute to, a genuinely corporate and Spirit-led church life. We see this as a necessary implication of the spiritual renewal of the church, and suspect that few yet realise either how important it is or how far it needs to go. Meanwhile, we welcome the preliminary experiments whereby both 'charismatic' and 'non-charismatic' Christians are currently seeking to discover for themselves what this principle might mean in practice.

3) Leadership and appointments. We believe a clergyman must see himself as an enabler and trainer of others to be the body of Christ in the place where they are. When the members of a church are renewed and revived so that they begin to exercise their gifts and to discover and develop their ministries, and lay leadership begins to grow, the pastor's work of oversight, teaching and leadership, and his function as a resource person, though changing perhaps in outward form, becomes more, not less, vital.

Accordingly, we believe that when the living becomes vacant in the charismatically-experienced church, great care must be taken that the functioning body of Christ in that place has a significant voice in the making of the next appointment. It also becomes important that a man be appointed who will gladly and skillfully lead a team, rather than expect to exercise a one-man pattern of ministry. This is just to say that the church, in making such an appointment, must keep up with what the Holy Spirit has been doing in that place, and not risk quenching him by ignoring, under-valuing or seeking to counter his work.

d) Keeping churches and congregations together. We have no new magical formula to hold churches together; there is only the old one of shared truth and mutual love, humility, tolerance and respect. Where churches split over these or any other matters, there are usually faults on both sides. Important guidelines will include: avoidance of any idea of first and second class Christians, which would engender pride, resentment and stubborn self-justification; willingness by those on all sides to respect each other's convictions, with openness to correction in the light of an honest reading of the New Testament; avoidance of quenching genuine spiritual gifts; respect for the authority of

131

official leaders in the local church; and avoidance of splinter groups developing whose focus is something other (and therefore less) than Jesus Christ himself.

We also believe it important that those who disagree on these or other matters should be brought together in direct encounter face-to-face, rather than talking about each other without meeting to discuss their differences.

e) Roman Catholics and renewal. The renewing work of the Holy Spirit has led to Christians of different backgrounds having fellowship together in Christ and in the Spirit, as old prejudices and dividing barriers melt under the new power of God's love in their lives. Protestants and Roman Catholics often associate with each other in this way. We welcome this, but at the same time recognize these dangers:

  i) A unity based on experience at the expense of doctrine would be less than the unity envisaged in the New Testament and would be dangerous in the long term.

 ii) Personal (and even corporate) renewal has not always meant the dropping of all anti-biblical or sub-biblical traditions and practices. We see the need to pray for and to encourage reformation by God's word as well as renewal by his Spirit in all churches.

In the case of the Roman Catholic Church, however, a massive international community which has only recently begun to question its own historic stances, we recognize that God calls us to be realistic in our expectations, and to allow time (how long is not for us to say) for the forces of reformation and renewal to operate widely enough for changes in official formulations and interpretations of doctrine to become possible, where they are necessary.

5. *Spiritual gifts*

a) Their nature, range and variety. A spiritual gift is a God-given capacity to serve others by his grace in a manner that edifies them in some way by the showing forth of Christ and his

132

love. Spiritual gifts are listed in Romans 12, 1 Corinthians 12, Ephesians 4 and 1 Peter 4. We see no biblical warrant for isolating one set of gifts from other gifts listed elsewhere in the New Testament, nor for treating these lists as exhaustive.

Neither the context and terminology of 1 Corinthians 12 nor a comparison of the lists themselves will allow us to elevate one gift or set of gifts above another, although Paul indicates that in a meeting prophecy edifies the church, whereas tongues without interpretation do not. The comparative value of gifts depends upon the degree to which they edify, in the context in which they operate. Whilst observing that not all gifts and ministries have been equally in evidence throughout the Church's history, we declare our openness to receiving any spiritual gifts that are consonant with the New Testament, and see no reason why such gifts should not be given and exercised today. A few which have sometimes caused particular difficulties are singled out for special treatment later.

b) Praying for gifts. The Holy Spirit is sovereign in the distribution of gifts to particular individuals. The New Testament encourages the congregation to desire and to pray for spiritual gifts and to exercise those received for the good of others. A congregation may rightly pray expectantly for the Lord to supply a need, and where they see a gift or ministry required to meet that need, it is clearly appropriate to ask him for it.

c) Gifts for every member. The New Testament teaches that every Christian has already received some gift or gifts, and lays upon all the responsibility to recognize what is already given, and to manifest it. It also encourages all to desire, and therefore be open to receive and exercise, a spiritual gift and ministry of one sort or another, and sees the healthy functioning of a congregation as the body of Christ as dependent upon each one contributing in this way.

We believe this to be one of the most important truths highlighted by the charismatic movement, with far-reaching implications for the life and ministry of all our churches.

d) Their use, regulation and oversight. We believe it is vital that those who claim to have gifts should have those gifts tested by the leadership in the body of Christ in that place, and not be given *carte blanche* to exercise them as if above being questioned or corrected. Christians with recognized gifts should not be stifled, but rather encouraged in their ministry by the leadership. The exercise of gifts must be overseen by the eldership of the churches and by those more experienced in that field. Such gifts should be kept within the fellowship of the church, and not become a focal-point for a new 'gift-centred' fellowship.

6. *On particular gifts and ministries*

a) Apostleship. Who, if any, of the first Christians shared the authority belonging to the Eleven and Paul, and on what grounds, may be debatable, but there is little doubt as to what that authority was. Through divine revelation and inspiration these men were authoritative spokesmen for, witnesses to, and interpreters of, God and his Son.

Their personal authority as teachers and guides—authority bestowed and guaranteed by the risen Christ—was final, and no appeal away from what they said was allowable. Such authority now belongs only to the scripture of the Old and New Testaments, under which all our churches and church leaders stand. Though latter-day ministries may in certain respects parallel apostolic functions, yet in their primary role as authoritative instructors the apostles have no successors, and any utterances or gestures of leadership today for which immediate inspiration is claimed must be evaluated by appeal to apostolic standards set forth in Holy Scripture. This is the Church's one sure safeguard against being spiritually tyrannised and misled, as has repeatedly happened in church history.

b) Prophecy. While estimates and interpretations of the New Testament phenomenon of prophecy vary, it is not identified there with the gift and ministry of teaching. Immediacy in receiving and declaring God's present message to men is the hallmark of New Testament prophecy, as of its Old Testament counterpart. Preaching may at times approximate more to prophecy, although its basic character is one of teaching and exhortation.

If the possibility of prophecy in the sense of speaking a word from the Lord under the direct prompting of the Holy Spirit is admissible today, what is said will be tested by its general agreement with scripture, and will not be accepted as adding materially to the Bible's basic revelation of God and his saving purposes in Christ. It will not be required that such utterances be cast in the first person singular, nor will those that are so cast be thought to have greater authority on that account.

c) Miracles. The living God is revealed to us in scripture as the Creator and Sustainer of all things, whose normal mode of operation is through the processes of nature and history, which he controls. We think there is need to unfold this truth more thoroughly at the present time, teaching Christians to discern the hand of God in all things. At the same time we all believe miracles can occur today. Despite the virtual impossibility of arriving at a satisfactory definition of 'miracles' in strictly scientific terms, we are in general agreement concerning their nature and purpose. We follow scripture in conceiving of miracles phenomenally, as occurrences of an unusual kind which bring awareness of the close presence of God, working out his will of salvation or judgment according to his word, and seeking by these manifestations to stir up the observers and beneficiaries (not to mention others) to new trust and worship. We believe that faith in the living God as delineated in scripture compels us to be open to the possibility of miracles in every age under the New Covenant, and that the Lord may call some Christians to particular ministries of a more obviously miraculous kind in particular times and places.

However we are never in a position to demand a miracle, since we may never dictate to our sovereign Lord how he shall work in answer to our prayers. Our business is to rest upon and claim his promises in obedience to his word, but to leave the means of the answer to his wisdom.

Over-concentration upon the miraculous can blind people to the manifold and wonderful everyday working of God in the world in 'non-miraculous' ways in the spheres of both creation and history. On the precise degree of expectation of miracles which is appropriate today we are not, however, completely agreed.

d) Healing. We belive that all true wholeness, health and healing come from God. We do not therefore regard 'divine healing' as being always miraculous. God's normal mode of healing is through the processes he has built into the human body and spirit. We also look forward to the resurrection, knowing that only then shall we be finally and fully freed from sickness, weakness, pain and mortality. At the same time we welcome the recovery by the Church of a concern for healing, and rejoice at those who have found new psychological or physical health through faith in Christ, and through Christian ministries and gifts of healing. But we also wish to express caution against giving wrong impressions and causing unnecessary distress through (i) making it appear that it is sinful for a Christian to be ill; (ii) laying too great a stress and responsibility upon the faith of the individual who is seeking healing; (iii) emphasising physical health more than the wholeness of the person; and (iv) setting non-medically-trained ministries and gifts of healing in opposition to the work and ministry of doctors and nurses.

e) Exorcism. Part of the ministry of Jesus Christ in the New Testament and in every age around the world is to set people free from the grip of satanic forces at work in or upon their personality. We are united in our belief in the existence of such personal spiritual powers, and in both the need and the possibility of Christ's deliverance. For he has been exalted far above all principalities and powers, and God has put them all under his feet. We all can testify that the regular ministry of word and sacrament, together with the prayer of faith which this evokes, can liberate people from bondage to the power of the devil. Sometimes, however, especially in clear cases of demon possession, exorcism may be necessary.

While not doubting that Christ gives to some people especially the necessary gifts to exercise this ministry safely and effectively in his name, it is an area fraught with dangers, which drive us to utter several cautionary warnings: (i) a preoccupation with demons (often to the neglect of the holy angels) is generally both dangerous and unbalanced, as is the tendency to attribute every unusual condition to demonic influence or presence; (ii) it is wise to avoid speaking of 'spirits' or 'demons' to those to whom we minister personally, unless this is absolutely unavoidable; (iii) the ministry of exorcism should not normally be exercised either by any Christian alone, or by any Christians without proper authority and oversight within the church; (iv) persons in need of this ministry will frequently need help at the psychological/emotional level of healing as well; (v) consultation with medical opinion (preferably sympathetic to a Christian viewpoint) is always highly desirable; (vi) careful pastoral follow-up is essential.

f) Speaking in tongues. Many Christians today testify to the value of this gift in their experience. Opinions vary as to how much of modern glossolalia corresponds with the New Testament phenomenon. Most of us would accept that some tongues-speaking, though not necessarily a heavenly language, is nevertheless divinely given and has spiritual and psychological value. We are also aware that a similar phenomenon can occur under occult/demonic influence, and that some such utterances may be merely psychological in origin and not necessarily edifying or beneficial at all.

Opinions also vary as to the value of this gift to the individual, and (with interpretation) to the church. We consider it necessary to hold to the balance of the New Testament in our general attitude to it, in accordance with 1 Corinthians 14, neither exalting it above all other gifts, nor despising it and forbidding its exercise (though always with interpretation if in public).

But if we are true to the New Testament we shall seek to test it, as we do the other gifts in their public exercise, by its edifying effects; and we shall regulate its use scripturally, encouraging believers with this gift to 'pray with the understanding also' both in public and in private.

CONCLUSION: THE GOAL OF RENEWAL

The goal of renewal is not merely renewed individuals but a renewed and revived Church, alive with the life of Christ, subject to the word of Christ, filled with the Spirit of Christ, fulfilling the ministry of Christ, constrained by the love of Christ, preaching the good news of Christ, and thrilled in its worship by the glory of Christ.

Such a Church alone can adequately portray Jesus Christ to the world. In preaching, writing and counselling, the Christ-centredness of the Christian life and the work of the Holy Spirit must constantly be emphasised, so that we may all together grow up fully into him, our glorious Head.

APPENDIX C
REPORT ON THE
1976
CHARISMATIC
LEADERS
CONFERENCE
U.S.A.

Reconciliation among major segments of the charismatic renewal resulted from a week-long meeting of ministers, teachers, and editors in Oklahoma City March 8-12, 1976. Thirty-eight representatives from the movement gathered at the Center for Christian Renewal for four days of prayer, sharing, and discussion on the shepherding-discipleship-submission controversy that has troubled Christians in many parts of the world in the last year.

The censensus of the meeting was that allegations of heresy were unfounded, that there was no reason to question the integrity of the teachers involved, and that, while many doctrinal differences remain among the groups represented, those differences fall within acceptable limits.

The conferees agreed that much of the controversy had grown out of rumor and misunderstanding, misapplication of certain scriptural principles, and a lack of communication among leaders of different ministries and groups.

Leaders associated with Christian Growth Ministries, Ft. Lauderdale, Florida, around whom much of the controversy has swirled, said in a statement to the conference that they regretted the abuse and confusion that had resulted from the discipleship teaching. They pledged to correct such abuses and misunderstandings wherever possible.

Other groups represented at the conference—the fifth meeting in a series beginning in Seattle in 1971—were as follows:

American Baptist Charismatic Fellowship, Catholic Charismatic Renewal Service Committee, Church of the Redeemer (Episcopal), Classical Pentecostals, Elim Fellowship, Episcopal Charismatic Fellowship, Logos International Fellowship, Lutheran Charismatic Renewal Service Commitee, Mennonite Renewal Services, Presbyterian Charismatic Communion, World Missionary Assistance Plan, Youth with a Mission, and various Christian centers and ministries from every geographical area of the United States and Canada.

Specifically the conference:

1. Accepted the report from a theological inquiry into the discipleship-shepherding teaching held in Ann Arbor, Michigan, in December 1975.

2. Received and commended a statement of concern and regret issued by the teachers associated with Christian Growth Ministries.

3. Called for an end to public attacks and malicious gossip as a way of dealing with differences within the Christian community.

4. Adopted a statement of ethics for handling differences between ministers, which was drawn up as a result of the meeting in Seattle in 1971.

5. Established a "Charismatic Concerns Committee" to plan future conferences and to help deal with issues and problems that arise in the charismatic renewal.

6. Agreed to continue to meet together at least annually, to consider how the charismatic renewal can best serve the renewal of the church.

THE ANN ARBOR REPORT

Following are the main elements of the report from the Ann Arbor meeting:

December 16-17, 1975, a group of us met in Ann Arbor,

Michigan, for theological and pastoral evaluation of the current controversy over "discipleship" and "shepherding."

We took up the questions which are most frequently raised:

- the extent of authority and submission
- tithing to a shepherd
- the relationship between "sheep" and "shepherd"— how extensive?
- the influence of the teachers from Ft. Lauderdale
- trans-local authority, the possibility of a new denomination

We experienced a real measure of understanding. We do not mean that there are not differences which still remain, for there are. But they need not be differences which divide us. In fact, we have come to a great sense of unity in the Spirit. We believe that where there have been excesses and abuses, they can be corrected . . . . We have come to the conviction that a considerable measure of the controversy has resulted from misunderstanding and poor communication. The real differences which exist are well within the bounds of "allowable variety" in the Body of Christ.

. . . . We reached the place which could be best described as a "committed relationship" to one another. This does not mean that we do or will agree with one another in all regards, but it does mean that we are not justified in publicly attacking the motivation, the attitude, the view, the conduct of one another without endeavoring to bring about a reconciliation through the prescribed New Testament procedure as outlined in Matthew 18, in love. It is anticipated that this "committed relationship" will increase in depth and in numbers among those who have been given responsibility in the charismatic renewal . . . .

Respectfully submitted by:

Brick Bradford	Kilian McDonnell
Jamie Buckingham	Bob Mumford
Larry Christenson	Derek Prince

Steve Clark
David du Plessis
Everett Fullam
Dan Malachuk

Kevin Ranaghan
Michael Scanlon
Charles Simpson
Rodman Williams

(Note: *Logos Journal* and *New Wine* magazines have published in their March 1976 issues a Question-and-Answer Forum in which some of the teachers associated with Christian Growth Ministries provided clarification on the discipleship-shepherding issues.)

STATEMENT OF CONCERN AND REGRET

Following is the statement issued in Oklahoma City by teachers associated with Christian Growth Ministries:

We realize that controversies and problems have arisen among Christians in various areas as a result of our teaching in relation to subjects such as submission, authority, discipling, shepherding. We deeply regret these problems and insofar as they are due to fault on our part, we ask forgiveness from our fellow believers whom we have offended.

We realize that our teachings, though we believed them to be essentially sound, have in various places been misapplied or handled in an immature way; and that this has caused problems for our brothers in the ministry. We deeply regret this and ask for forgiveness. Insofar as it lies in our power, we will do our best to correct these situations and to restore any broken relationships.

Don Basham
Ern Baxter
Bob Mumford
John Poole
Derek Prince
Charles Simpson

RESPONSE TO STATEMENT

The remaining conferees received with gratitude the above statement from the teachers associated with Christian Growth Ministries and thereafter the entire conference made the following response:

We call for an end to the public attacks on those individuals involved in the teaching under question. Public attacks of this kind are a grave disservice to the work of Christ. Also, the multitude of rumors and stories of alleged or actual abuses that are being circulated by members of the Body at large are doing serious harm to His Kingdom.

We appeal to all Christians to live according to the teaching of Scripture which relates to resolving difficulties between members of the Body. In particular, we reaffirm, and invite all Christian leaders to affirm, the following guidelines based on Matthew 18:15-17, as a statement of how we desire to relate to one another when difficult situations arise. These guidelines were originally drawn up after the Seattle meeting in 1971.

1. We believe that God has set us in positions of leadership within the Body of Christ, either as leaders within a local congregation, or as preachers with a ministry to the Body of Christ at large, or in a combination of both these ministries.

2. So far as we are able, we will seek at all times to keep our lives and ministries sound in respect to ethics, morals and doctrine.

3. We will acknowledge and respect all others who have similar ministries and who are willing to make a similar commitment in respect to ethics, morals and doctrine.

4. If at any time we have any criticism or complaint against any of our brother ministers within the Body of Christ, we will seek to take the following steps: First, we will approach our brother directly and privately, and seek to establish the true facts. Second, if thereafter we still find grounds for criticism or complaint, we will seek the counsel and cooperation of at least two other ministers mutually acceptable to our brother and

ourselves, in order to make any changes needed to rectify the situation. Finally, if this does not resolve the criticism or complaint, we will seek to bring the whole matter before a larger group of our fellow ministers, or alternately before the local congregation to which our brother belongs. In following these steps, our motive will be to retain the fellowship of our brother and to arrive at a positive, scriptural solution which will maintain the unity of the Body of Christ.

5. Until we have done everything possible to follow the steps outlined in paragraph 4, we will not publicly voice any criticism or complaint against a fellow minister.

6. In our general conduct towards our fellow ministers and all other believers, we will seek to obey the exhortation of scripture to "follow after the things which make for peace and things wherewith one may edify another" (Romans 14:19).

Don Basham
Ern Baxter
Brick Bradford
Jack Brombach
Larry Christenson
Steve Clark
Dick Coleman
Judson Cornwall
Loren Cunningham
David du Plessis
David Edwards
Charles Farah
Everett Fullam
Joe Garlington
James Hamann
Bob Hawn
Rod Lensch
Len LeSourd
Nelson Litwiller

Francis MacNutt
Ralph Mahoney
Ralph Martin
Earl Morey
Bob Mumford
Ken Pagard
Don Pfotenhauer
John Poole
Derek Prince
Lester Pritchard
Kevin Ranaghan
Jeff Schiffmayer
Charles Simpson
Bob Slosser
Vinson Synan
Morris Vaagenes
Bob Whitaker
Maxwell Whyte
Bruce Yocum

NOTES

1. Anthony Sampson, *The Seven Sisters* (New York: Bantam, 1976).
2. Richard Quebedeaux, *The Young Evangelicals* (New York: Harper and Row, 1974).
3. Quebedeaux, p. 40.
4. J. D. Douglas, editor, *Let the Earth Hear His Voice* (Minneapolis: World Wide Publications, 1975), pp. 4, 5.
5. Clark Pinnock, "The New Pentecostalism: Reflection of a Well-wisher," *Christianity Today*, September 14, 1973.
6. Walter Hollenweger, *The Pentecostals* (Minneapolis: Augsburg, 1972).
7. *Crusade*, October 1976 (printed in England).
8. Bill McSweeney, *The Times*, October 16, 1976 (printed in London, England).
9. Leon J. Suenens, *A New Pentecost?* (New York: Seabury, 1977), p. 119.
10. Suenens, p. 5.
11. This paper has since merged with *Logos Journal*, a publication of the same publisher, Logos International, Plainfield, N.J.
12. John R. Stott, *Baptism and Fullness: The Work of the Holy Spirit Today* (Downers Grove, Ill.: InterVarsity Press, 1976), p. 26.
13. Simon Tugwell, *Did You Receive the Spirit?* (New York: Paulist Press, 1973), p. 47.
14. James G. Dunn, *Baptism in the Holy Spirit* (Philadelphia: Westminster, 1977).
15. David C. K. Watson, *One in the Spirit* (England: Hodder and Stoughton, 1973).
16. Suenens, p. 80.
17. Michael Green, *Renewal*, No. 53 (October/November 1975), p. 14 (printed in England). See also Green's book *I Believe in the Holy Spirit* (Grand Rapids, Mich.: Eerdmans, 1975), pp. 142-147.
18. Thomas A. Smail, *Reflected Glory* (Grand Rapids, Mich.: Eerdmans, 1976).
19. Michael Harper, *Power for the Body of Christ* (Plainfield, N.J.: Logos, 1973). Although this book was written in 1964 in the formulative stage of the development of my thinking, it still substantially reflects my present (1978) view of this matter.
20. See particularly Dennis and Rita Bennett's *The Holy Spirit and You* (Plainfield, N.J.: Logos, 1971).

21. Dr. Martyn Lloyd-Jones, "Quenching the Holy Spirit," *Westminster Record*, September 1969 (printed in England).

22. Kilian McDonnell, editor, *The Holy Spirit and Power* (New York: Doubleday, 1975). See also *The Baptism in the Holy Spirit as an Ecumenical Problem* by McDonnell and Arnold Bittlinger (South Bend, Ind.: Charismatic Renewal Services, 1972). On pp. 52, 53 of McDonnell's book *The Baptism in the Holy Spirit as an Ecumenical Problem* there is a helpful summary. It shows how McDonnell's thinking is based on the one initiation concept, which is larger than water baptism but denies a so-called "second blessing." He identifies two (not one) traditions in the New Testament: the Lukan and the Pauline-Johannine. But for both of them, "baptism in the Holy Spirit is another name for the rite of initiation." He goes on to write, *"baptism in the Holy Spirit manifests itself in an adult when by either a crisis act or a growth process he says yes to what objectively took place during the rite of initiation."* The italics are mine. These quotations show how close differing viewpoints often are to one another.

23. David Watson, *I Believe in Evangelism* (Grand Rapids, Mich.: Eerdmans, 1977), p. 166.

24. Jeanne Harper and Betty Pulkingham, editors, *Sound of Living Waters* (Grand Rapids, Mich.: Eerdmans, 1977); *Fresh Sounds* (Grand Rapids, Mich.: Eerdmans, 1976).

25. Ralph Martin, *Unless the Lord Builds the House* (Notre Dame, Ind.: Ave Maria Press, 1971).

26. Stephen Clark, editor, *Team Manual for the Life in Spirit Seminars* (South Bend, Ind: Charismatic Renewal Services, 1971).

27. *The Nottingham Statement* (England: Falcon, 1977), p. 20. It was interesting as a participant at both the Keele Congress 1967 and the Nottingham Congress 1977 to compare the effect the charismatic movement had on both. At Keele the subject was very much taboo; yet nearly everyone was talking privately about it. Speakers avoided the subject, but it was obviously in people's minds. By 1977, only ten years later, the subject was being talked about freely in public, but very little in private, a complete reversal of attitudes.

28. In my book *Let My People Grow* (Plainfield, N.J.: Logos, 1977), I have gone extensively into the question of "every-member ministry," and attempted to expose the modern curse of professionalism. The response to the book has been interesting in that nearly every stream of the Church, if one judges by book reviews and press comments, basically agrees on the principles, though differing on the details.

29. *Nottingham Statement*, pp. 20, 32, 33.

30. Jamie Buckingham, *Daughter of Destiny* (Plainfield, N.J.: Logos, 1976).

31. Michael Harper, *Spiritual Warfare* (Plainfield, N.J.: Logos, 1973). A much more detailed and thorough book on the subject which I can highly recommend is: John Richards, *But Deliver Us from Evil* (New York: Seabury, 1974).

32. Juan Carlos Ortiz and Jamie Buckingham, *Call to Discipleship* (Plainfield, N.J.: Logos, 1975).